Chinese Landscape Painting for Beginners

Li Dongxu

Translated by Wen Jingen with Pauline Cherrett

FOREIGN LANGUAGES PRESS

First Edition 2007
Second Printing 2009

Text by Li Dongxu
English translation by Wen Jingen with Pauline Cherrett
Designed by Cai Rong
Art by Li Dongxu, Sun Shuming and Wen Jingen

Chinese Landscape Painting for Beginners

ISBN 978-7-119-04615-0

Published by Foreign Languages Press
24 Baiwanzhuang Road, Beijing, 100037, China
Home page: http://www.flp.com.cn
Email address: info@flp.com.cn
sales@flp.com.cn
Distributed by China International Book Trading Corporation
35 Chegongzhuang Xilu, Beijing 100044, China
P. O. Box 399, Beijing, China

Printed in the People's Republic of China

Contents

Translator's notes:

1. All illustrations in this book were executed and provided by the author unless otherwise stated. 书中未注明作者的图片均为本书作者所作。

2. To make this book more accessible for non-Chinese readers, the translator has extensively edited the original text, and added some illustrations. The translator, and not the author, is responsible for all errors accruing from the rewriting and rearrangement of art.

为适应外国读者需要，本书编译过程中对原作的图文做了一定改动。着粪续貂，在所难免；所生舛误，咎在译者。敬希作者及读者见谅。

Introduction

Wen Jingen

This manual is specially prepared for the Western reader who is interested in Chinese painting. I assume he or she will already have some interests in the art of painting in general, and also may have viewed some Chinese paintings as originals or prints. As he or she embarks on learning more about this fascinating art form, I (as the translator of this book) have taken liberties to alter some of the paragraphs and illustrations, and would like to offer some suggestions which I hope will be useful.

It is agreed that Chinese painting prior to the 20th century had achieved great success in landscape. Needless to say to engage in such a genre, either wholeheartedly or in a dilettantish way, is an exciting experience.

Painting from Life, by Wen Jingen

But soon the reader encounters a problem: how to approach Chinese landscape? Naturally, to produce a Chinese painting the artist must use instruments and materials that are quite different from those used for oil painting. Let a new hand who has received training in drawing and oil painting use a Chinese brush, ink and colour to produce a painting on Chinese paper, and the result will be a good landscape but does not look like a "Chinese" painting at all. Obviously, to produce a Chinese landscape using Chinese tools alone, is not enough.

Chinese painting with a long history of development is fully mature, both technically and theoretically. There are mountains of theoretical works dealing with landscape (only a very small portion has been translated into English) and there are as many approaches as there are art historians. For those who do not know the Chinese language, they are out of reach. But even for those who know Chinese, they often puzzle rather than enlighten — even Chinese students of art are often baffled by the abstruse, "philosophical" terms in them. Not that those terms are wrong, but they do involve complicated concepts and hence are difficult for beginners.

In my opinion, however abstract the idea, it can be illustrated by referring to its "physical" aspects and to people's direct experiences. However different Western and Chinese arts appear from each other, they have some elementary things in common. Now I will try to describe Chinese landscape from a concrete, tangible viewpoint. I hope this will give the reader some enlightenment and a good starting point.

The Eye

People tend to believe a picture executed "from life" can be an accurate image of the real world. In his *Art and Illusion* (pp.84-85), E. H. Gombrich shows us two pictures of the same spot; one is done by an unknown Romanist artist and the other by the Chinese artist Chiang Yee.

Derwentwater by unknown artist

Derwentwater by Chiang Yee

Gombrich ascribes the difference in rendering to the different methods used by the artists. An artist learns the "vocabulary" of a language of art and when he produces a painting, he chooses motifs that can be rendered in his style. The scenery painted by the Chinese artist is what he sees through "Chinese eyes". Physically, we cannot prove that what is projected on the retina of a Chinese artist is different from what is projected on the retina of a Western artist. Their paintings are different because their eyes are selective in different ways. An artist acquires a language of art through viewing paintings and also through copying or imitating pictures available to him, from exhibitions, from printed albums or from his textbooks. (Some artists do not copy, but nearly all artists at their early stage of study consciously or unconsciously imitate masterpieces.) An idiom of the Chinese language of art is illustrated by the comparison of Chiang Yee's painting with Shen Zhou's landscape — Chinese artists' preference for expressive empty space in painting and Western artists' penchant for physically tangible space. Also, where the Western artist sees the reflection of mountains in water, the Chinese artist sees sinuous lines that suggest ripples on the water surface. While a Western landscape offers an illusion of a real three-dimensional area which the viewer can enter, a Chinese landscape leaves empty or ill-defined areas waiting to be filled in by the viewer's imagination. Chiang

Landscape (detail) by Shen Zhou (1427-1509)

Yee must have cultivated his "eye" by viewing and probably copying other Chinese artists' works.

Apart from seeing empty spaces or areas with sparse strokes in a painting, a Chinese landscape artist often "sees" a scene from unfixed locations. A Chinese landscape does not display what the artist sees when standing at a fixed position. Instead, it usually displays, as it were, what the artist sees along the way he has travelled. The 19th-century engraving of Cathedral of Notre Dame in Chartres and a modern photo of the same building, taken from Gombrich's *Art and Illusion*, p. 72,

Cathedral of Notre Dame in Chartres, 19th-century engraving

Cathedral of Notre Dame in Chartres, modern photograph

show that we can capture (though with discrepancy in proportions of details — perhaps due to repairing of part of the building) with a camera the same picture viewed by a Western artist. But one cannot shoot a picture like Du Qiong's *Landscape*. We would need many cameras to take different parts of the scene and then put them together. Yet there is no guarantee for success: the lack of footholds may abort our endeavour. In other words, a Western landscape usually presents one field of vision while a Chinese view presents many visions simultaneously. The Chinese artist looks with his mind's eye! This may help to clarify the difference in composition of Chinese and Western landscapes.

The Western landscape is "physically" realistic while the Chinese landscape is less true to the images projected on to our lens but more faithful to our mental experiences. That is why ancient Chinese people compared viewing landscape paintings at home to "a journey while lying in bed" (*wo you* 卧游).

If an artist constantly views Chinese landscape masterpieces and practises, he will acquire a "Chinese eye". With that "Chinese eye" he will learn to put plural visions into one picture and his landscape will become more and more "Chinese".

Landscape by Du Qiong

The Hand

With an understanding of the making of a Chinese landscape, an artist can place his brush onto the paper and paint a landscape. At the preparatory stage both Western and Chinese landscape artists do the same — they make a draft with a pencil, crayon or charcoal. But after this, their paths branch — the oil painter applies broad and narrow patches of colour on the canvas; the Chinese painter draws the depicted objects with ink strokes in various shades. A Chinese painting may be uncoloured, but cannot be done without ink. The ink lines are the "bones" of a Chinese painting. They play a role far more important than a means of contouring and a "black" colour. It is generally accepted that without proper brushwork a painting cannot be called Chinese.

The yellow dotted line shows the position of the brush tip; the red lines show the direction of the brush tip's movement.

Line is also used in Western art. Figures on Hellenic pottery are drawn with forceful lines. Jean Ingress enchanted the audience with neat and precise lineation. Designs of William Morris boast superb linear mode. What makes Chinese line different is that this line is produced with special attention paid to manipulating the brush tip. If the brush tip is kept at the centre of a stroke, the stroke looks full and vigorous. If the brush tip is kept at one side of a stroke, the stroke looks flat. The brush tip can be concealed within the stroke or left exposed at one or two ends of the stroke. By controlling the brush tip, one can produce a "round" or "square" stroke, etc. It seems to me that Western artists seldom pay attention to the position of the brush tip during the movement of the brush.It should not be difficult to keep the brush tip at certain positions, and sure enough a beginner can do this after a little practice.

A few of many possible types of strokes

Illustrations by Wen Jingen

Good brushwork means far more than the position of the brush tip — it should be resolute, energetic and spirited. It can take months or years to achieve good brushwork.

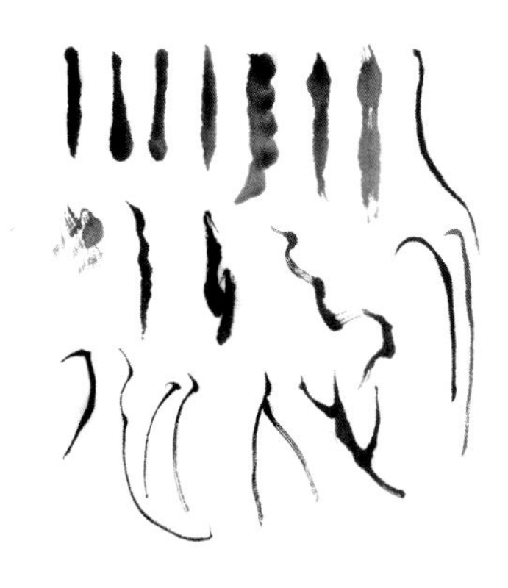

Good brushwork is certainly a benchmark for a masterly painting. This may also be true for Western art. Compare a masterpiece in a museum and its copy sold in a roadside cheap shop and you will feel the latter is of a much inferior quality. Both the original and its copy present the same image, but in the latter the vigour of its execution is absent.

Brushwork in Chinese painting has much in common with Chinese calligraphy. The relationship of painting and calligraphy has been an issue debated about for a long time. For a beginner, if you know the Chinese language and practise Chinese calligraphy, you will approach the brushwork more or less in the same way as a native Chinese. But if you do not know the Chinese language or Chinese calligraphy, you can still gain some insight into the Chinese brushwork by looking at the strokes in English calligraphy.

A few of many possible types of strokes

Illustrations by Wen Jingen

When you see a signature on an old manuscript in a library, you are impressed by the beauty of the strokes. You do not mind if a letter is a bit too long or short. The important thing is that the stroke must be done by a sure hand and in one movement. Retouching is undesirable. A person's calligraphy may divulge his personality — dashing handwriting is likely to be done by a resolute person, refined handwriting by an attentive person, and messy handwriting by a careless person, and so on. It is not difficult to tell the work of a well-trained hand and that of a new hand — the former shows confidence while the latter shows uncertainty.

You do not only examine individual letters, you evaluate the whole piece: you expect all the characters to be coherent. If some characters look weak or hesitant in a piece of calligraphy, you feel as if you hear a singer sing out of time or there is an undefined pause in the notation. It is here that Chinese calligraphers talk about the "strength" and "energy". If a character looks as if it is done by a sure hand, we say it contains strength. If a dancer is energetic her every move is vigorous and

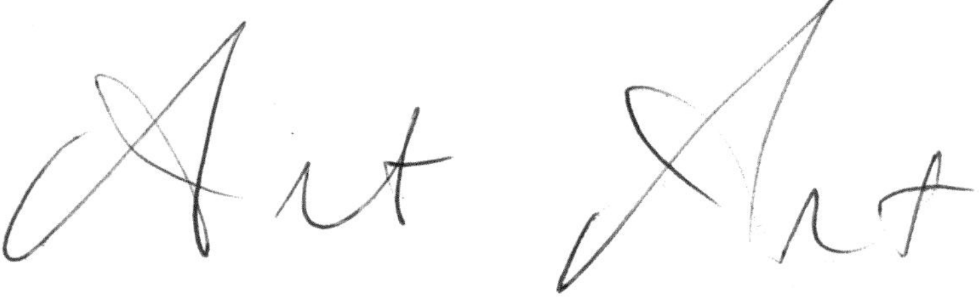

We prefer spontaneous calligraphy. Form does not matter as much as the "spirit".

Even if some characters are "imperfect", we do not like retouching. Retouching will make unsightly calligraphy.

Illustrations by Wen Jingen

continuous, otherwise she may totter or limp in some movements. In the same way, if the whole piece of calligraphy looks coherent, we say there is an "energy" running through it.

The same principles governs the Chinese calligraphy too. One also looks for the same thing in Chinese painting — the only difference is that handling a Chinese brush is more complicated than using a pen. Chinese brushwork is more sophisticated.

Before I learned English I could not tell a broadcast in English from a broadcast in German. To my ear they sounded equally "foreign". Later as I learned English, my ears became more and more sensitive to English pronunciation. Now I can tell British English from American English, and tell a London accent from a Birmingham accent. This means my sensitivity to English phonetics has been cultivated by reading, speaking and hearing English. Similarly, an artist will cultivate his sensitivity to brushwork through using the brush. Once he or she has learnt to control the brush tip, they will develop empathy into the brush, and become more and more sensitive to the quality of their own as well as others' brushwork.

Chinese painters apply "calligraphic" brushwork in their creation of paintings. They prefer sure-handed, forceful and energetic strokes. (Even if non-Chinese artists do not know Chinese or practise calligraphy, they may still achieve good brushwork). This is a long-standing tradition, but we cannot carry this principle too far. Some artists stress the quality of brushwork at the expense of form. After all, painting and calligraphy are two disciplines — one cannot substitute one with the other. A painting with good brushwork but poor form cannot be considered a successful one.

I hope my expounding of the brushwork will give the reader some insight. If my explanation is not helpful, the reader should skip over it and read the rest of the manual. As he or she learns the basic skills, and views more Chinese landscape paintings, there should be a better command of the brush. At the end of the day, there is nothing mysterious in Chinese painting!

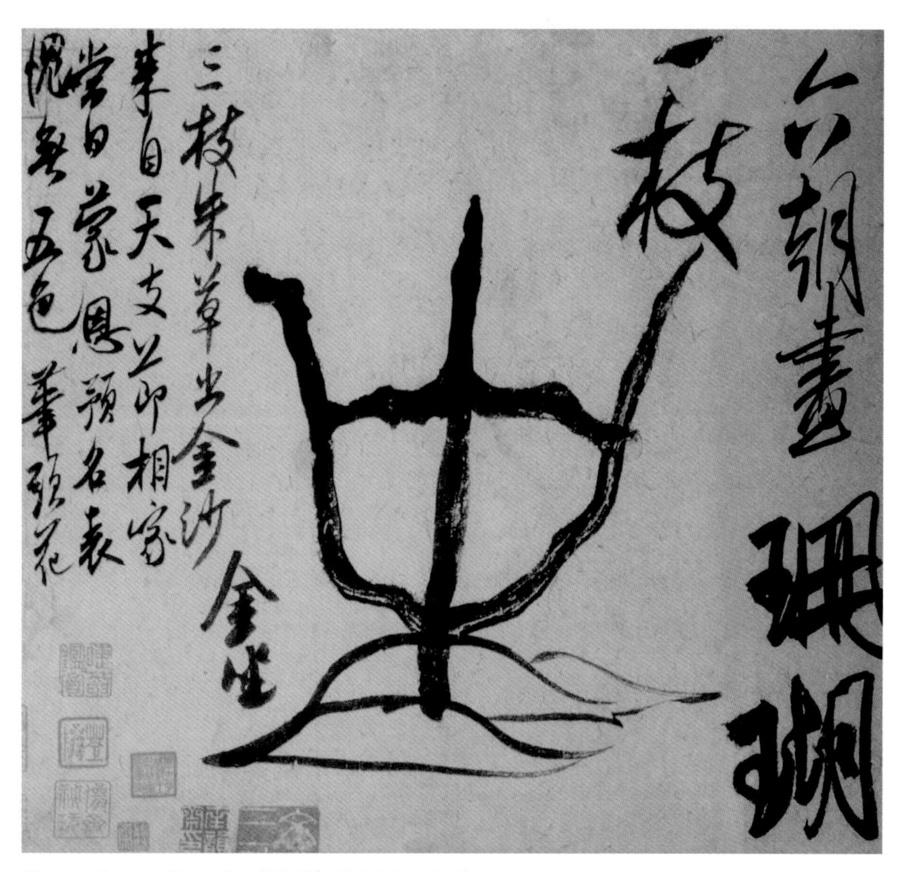

Coral Brush Rest by Mi Fu (1051-1107)
Picture or ideogram? The brushwork is perfect, but can you tell what this is? The painter intends to depict a brush-rest.

Inspiration

Once an artist learns the basic ideas of Chinese landscape, he needs inspiration for artistic creation. An ancient Chinese maxim goes that one "learns from nature meanwhile following his mind" (*wai shi zaohua, zhong fa xinyuan* 外师［師］造化;中法心源). The first half stresses observation of life and the latter half emphasises the mental treatment of what one sees.

During the last century in China, traditionalists advocated copying ancient works. Naturalists tended to negate the copyist tradition and preached painting from life. Both proposals have their advantages and limits. Here is a balanced view — in basic training one learns depiction skills by copying ancient works and in creation one draws inspiration from nature. Without copying former works, one's painting will lack the characteristics of Chinese painting. Without inspiration from nature, one cannot make innovation. This has been endorsed by many outstanding Chinese landscape artists' achievement in the last century. More aptly, Richard Edward says "Art is not a mirror but a discovery". (*Discovering Chinese Painting*, Kendall/ Hunt, 2000, p. 11)

For a beginner, learning brushwork and ink application skills from textbooks is necessary. But he must be aware that when an artist learns from tradition, he tends to acquire stereotypes (or in Gombrich's word, "schemata") which, like clichés in writing, are unavoidable. To infuse something new into one's art the artist must draw on life. Xu Beihong, a reformer of Chinese painting says, "The teacher of painting is not a model work but life itself." (*Benteng Chi Fu Jian* [Galloping on a Foot-long Picture], Baihua Wenyi Chubanshe, 2000, p. 67)

No Hard and Fast Rule in Art

So far, we have concerned ourselves with painting an up-to-the-standard Chinese landscape. This may be achievable for a non-Chinese artist but it is likely that his efforts may also result in something impure, a kind of hybrid. If this happens, it is not necessarily a bad thing. Hybridised art may have its special appeal. After all, there is no hard and fast rule in art.

Chinese Landscape — Mountain Water Painting

Landscape painting dates back a long time in China. Traditional Chinese landscape painting has been described as "Shan Shui Hua", literally meaning, "mountain water painting" — a name suggesting that the major motifs of the genre are mountains and water.

More than two thousand years ago, Confucius (roughly a contemporary of Plato) said "The wise people delight in waters and the benevolent people delight in mountains." Chinese people viewed a mountain as the symbol of longevity and water as the symbol of wealth, hence a landscape painting would often be featured in the centre of a wall facing the entrance to a salon.

One of the three major Chinese painting genres (the other two being figure and bird-and-flower), Chinese landscape painting emerged early in the development of painting in China. However, these landscape works often betrayed immaturity with disproportional human figures and natural forms. To be exact, landscape at that time usually served as a backdrop for figure paintings, and within the landscape a human figure might be painted larger than a mountain, or trees and rocks shown standing one by one like fingers on a hand. Chinese art historians agree that the earliest extant landscape painting is *Excursion in Spring* 游春图(圖) by Zhan Ziqian (active in late 6th century). The painting has been praised for its realistic presentation of "mountains and waters far and near in a foot-long picture that suggests a thousand-mile sight". The brilliantly coloured painting in blue and green, outlined with golden lines, portrays a sunny spring day with high ranking men and ladies on horseback enjoying the beautiful scene. This marks the beginning of landscape as an independent genre.

Excursion in Spring by Zhan Ziqian

Is the *Excursion in Spring* the original version or a copy?

The painting was recorded in an art history catalogue compiled six hundred years after the artist's time. Some connoisseurs doubted the authenticity of the painting. In fact few paintings of Zhan Ziqian's time have survived and most of the paintings attributed to that time are copies done by later artists. One view is that the painting may be a copy, but based on the original painting rather than a fake.

How different is Chinese "mountain and water" painting from Western landscape?

This discussion involves artistic and cultural issues. For a beginner, this subject may be reduced to two aspects — the technical and the conceptive. Technically, Chinese landscape is executed with Chinese brushes and ink on Chinese paper, all quite different from tools used by

Riverside Scene at Qingming Festival (detail) by Zhang Zeduan (dates unknown, active 1100-1125)

Western artists and all producing different results. In order to master these instruments, Chinese artists practise and study extensively. Ideologically, Chinese landscape painters also conceive a painting in a quite different way. For a Western painter, a landscape usually displays a scene that the artist can "see" without turning his or her head. Such a painting usually has one "focus" and in a way, one can record a similar vision with a camera. On the other hand a Chinese landscape painting represents what the artist "sees" when he or she tours around a place or many places. The painting is a composition of what is stored in the artist's head. There are usually many focuses in such a painting.

Mill by Jacob van Ruysdael (1628?-1682)

As you read this book and learn the painting skills step by step, you will have a better understanding of the different approach to landscape by Chinese and Western artists.

The "Four Treasures"

The brush, ink stick, ink stone and paper are the "four treasures" of the studio. They are indispensable for a painter or calligrapher.

Brush. Chinese brushes fall into three categories: those made from a stiff-fibre, those made from a soft-fibre and those made from mixed-fibres. The stiff-fibre brushes are made from the hair of weasel, hare, badger or pig. Famous names for such brushes are *shanshui* (山水 mountain and water), *yiwen* (衣纹[紋] clothing fold), *yejin* (叶[葉]筋 leaf vein), *shuhua* (书画[畫] calligraphy and painting), *lanzhu* (兰[蘭]竹 orchid and bamboo) and so on. The soft brushes made of goat's hair include *duibi* (对笔[對筆] brush for writing hanging couplet) and *changfeng yanghao* (长锋[長鋒]羊毫 long tip goat hair brush). The mixed-fibre brushes are made from both stiff and soft fibres. Usually the core of the brush is made of stiff fibres and the outer fibres are soft hair. Brushes often used in this category are *da baiyun* (大白云[雲] large white cloud), *zhong baiyun* (中白云[雲] medium white cloud) and *xiao baiyun* (小白云[雲] small white cloud), as well as *qi zi san yang* (七紫三羊 seven tenth purple hare and three tenth goat hair), *wu zi wu yang* (五紫五羊 five tenth purple hare and five tenth goat hair), etc. Mixed-fibre brushes are neither too stiff nor too soft. Their resilient head can contain plenty of liquid.

Photograph by Sun Shuming

A beginner need not buy many brushes. A few stiff, soft and mix-fibre brushes in different sizes will do. Stiff-fibre brushes are for outlining and applying texture-strokes while soft-fibre brushes are for adding dots and colouring. Brushes should not be too small.

Usually the tip and belly of a brush are used — avoid pressing the whole of the brush onto the paper.

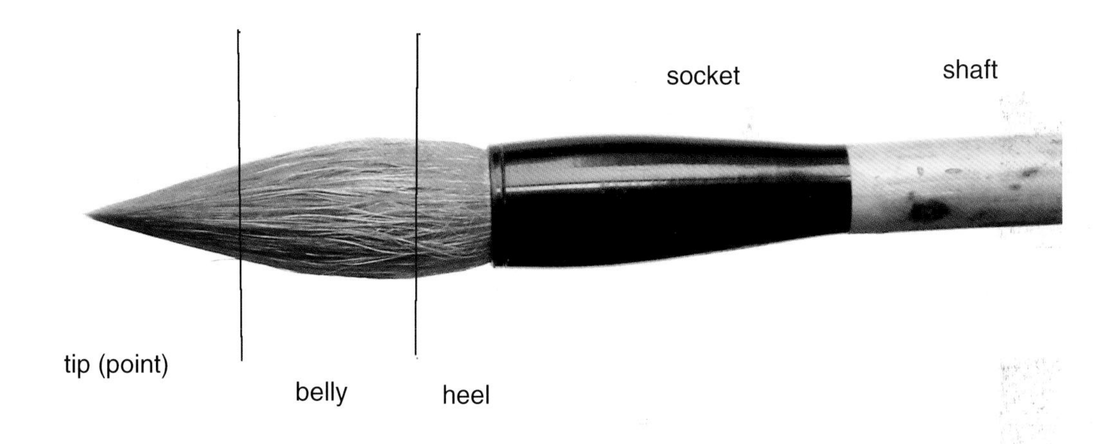

Illustration by Wen Jingen

Do not throw away your blunt brushes. As a rule, a sharp-pointed brush is handy. When a brush is worn due to repeated use, the tip becomes blunt. A brush with a blunt tip does poor calligraphy, but it serves well for dotting in landscape painting.

Four virtues (si de 四德) of a good brush: 1. it has a pointed tip when loaded; 2. the fibres are flush with each other when the tip is pressed flat; 3. it is a perfect cone; and 4. it is resilient.

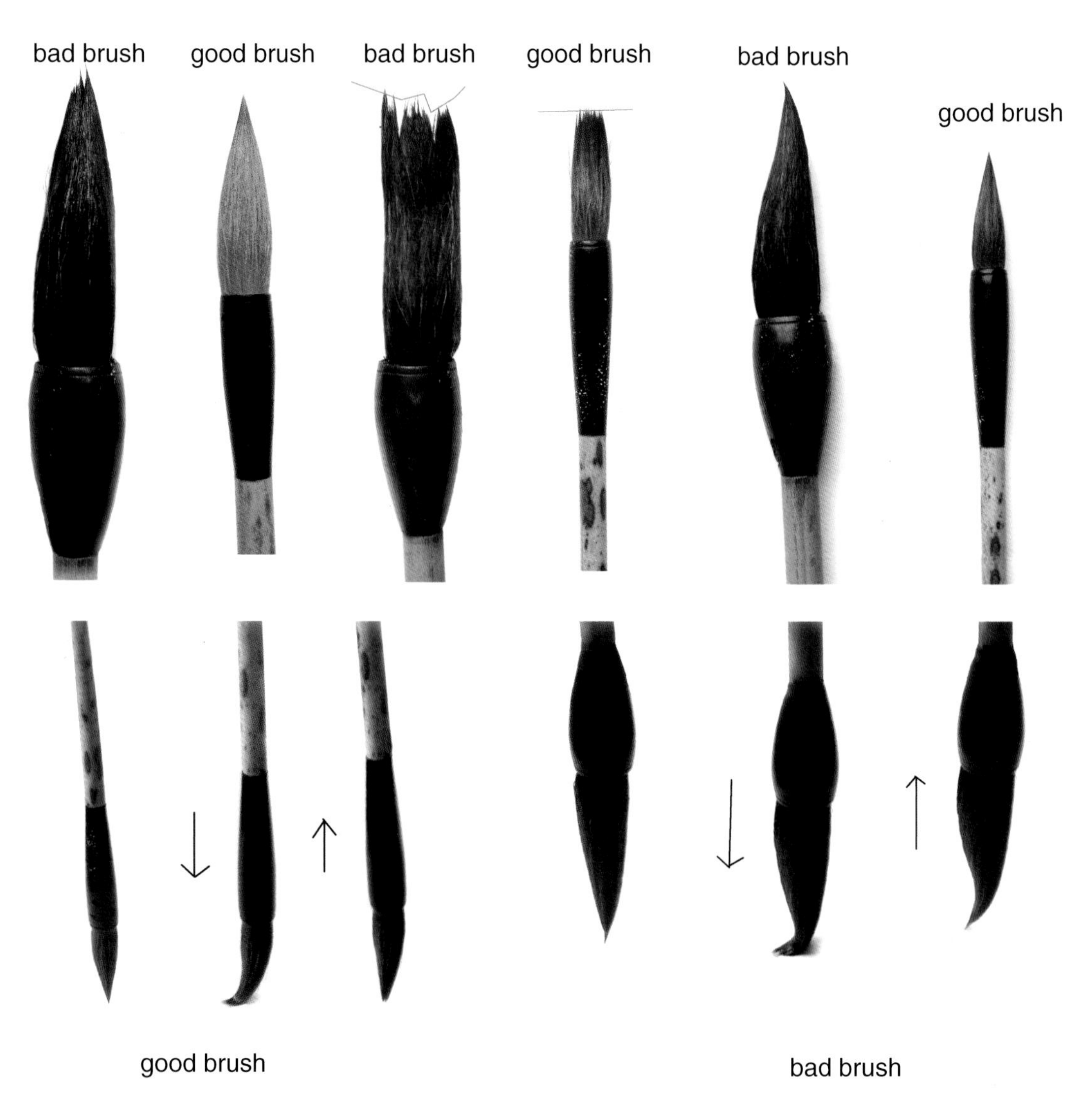

Illustration by Wen Jingen

Ink. The Chinese ink stick is made of soot collected from burning pinewood or tung oil. The ink stick produced with the former soot is called "song yan" (松烟[煙] pine soot) ink stick and the one produced with the latter soot, "you yan" (油烟[煙] oil soot) ink stick. "Oil soot" ink is bright and is good for painting landscape. You will learn to grind an ink stick on an ink stone to produce ink.

Bottled liquid ink is now available. Using bottled ink will save you grinding an ink stick. Choose the brands *zhonghua mozhi* (中华[華]墨汁 China ink), *yun tou yan mozhi* (云头艳[雲頭艷]墨汁) and *yi de ge mozhi* (一得阁[閣]墨汁 yi de ge ink). Bottled ink contains more glue than ink acquired by grinding an ink stick and so the brush loaded with

Photograph by Sun Shuming

bottled ink moves less freely. That's why some artists insist on using ink sticks instead of bottled ink. When the bottled ink is dry, the glue contained within it has evaporated. If you add water to the dry ink, the solution (known as "overnight ink") will contain sediment and is therefore best not used (although some artists deliberately use this "overnight ink" or even "week-old ink" for certain effects). Also when a painting produced with this ink is mounted, the ink marks may run and blur.

After you produce ink by grinding an ink stick, it is best to cover the ink stone with a lid. This prevents the ink from evaporating.

Paper. Today most Chinese landscape painters use a special paper called Xuan paper, sometimes erroneously known as "rice paper" in the West. Other types of Chinese paper may be used as well, such as bark, mulberry or leather paper. However, paper with a water-resistant, slippery surface like those used in computer printers or copy machines, is not suitable for Chinese landscape painting.

Unsized Xuan paper is absorbent, allowing ink and colour to run. This increases the expressiveness of the Chinese ink painting. Good unsized Xuan paper has the following virtues: 1. it shows clear traces of each brushstroke; 2. it keeps strokes of different shades distinct — when the ink and colour are dry, they will not fade; 3. it has proper permeability- water and ink do not spread too quickly or too slowly on it. Popular unsized Xuan papers are *jingpi* (净[凈]皮), *mianliao* (绵[綿]料), *liaoban* (料半), *yuban* (玉版) etc. There are both thick and thin papers available.

Sized Xuan paper has less permeability and water, ink etc. do not run. Sized paper is good for applying multilayer colour washes. It is used for the meticulous style painting like the blue and green landscape. Versions of sized paper include *chanyi* (蝉[蟬]翼 "cicada wing"), *fan mianlian* (矾棉连[連] "alumned soft"), qingshui (清水 "clear water"), *bingxue* (冰雪 "icy"), *yunmu* (云[雲]母 "mica"), and others.

Both sized and unsized silk may be used as a medium for Chinese painting. In fact it was widely used in the past. But as it is rather expensive I would not recommend it for beginners.

Ink stones. Ink stones are made of stone, pottery, clay, jade and metals. Some ink stones are elaborately carved and decorated — they are more for decoration than painting tools. For practical purposes, stone versions of the ink stones are best. Some of the best are *duan yan* (端砚[硯]) produced in Guangdong and *she yan* (歙砚[硯]) from Anhui. The "duan yan" stones are very expensive. A good ink stone is fine-grained, smooth and it should produce ink quickly. Also, to be practical, an ink stone should have a lid to prevent ink from evaporating and to keep it clean.

Inkstone, photograph by Wen Jingen

Nowadays bottled ink is widely used, and the ink stone is not as important as it used to be. However, you cannot achieve the extreme darkness with the bottled ink, so when you need "dried-up" ink, you will need to use an ink stick and ink stone.

Photograph by Sun Shuming

Colour. Colours for Chinese painting fall into two categories — mineral and vegetable colours. The vegetable colours (traditionally called, "herbal colours" *caose* 草色), include rattan yellow, indigo, rouge, etc. and the mineral colours ("stone colours" *shise* 石色) include ochre, cinnabar, azurite blue, malachite, vermilion, realgar, etc. Grinding clamshells makes a white power. Synthetic paints like zinc white and titanium white are also used today. The vegetable colours are water colours and the mineral colours are body colours.

Indigo (*huaqing* 花青). Usually it comes in a cake or flakes and contains glue. Before using, you should dissolve it with hot water. You can get green by mixing it with rattan yellow or purple by mixing it with red, and you can also mix it with ink.

Rattan yellow (*tenghuang* 藤黄). This is a poisonous pigment and

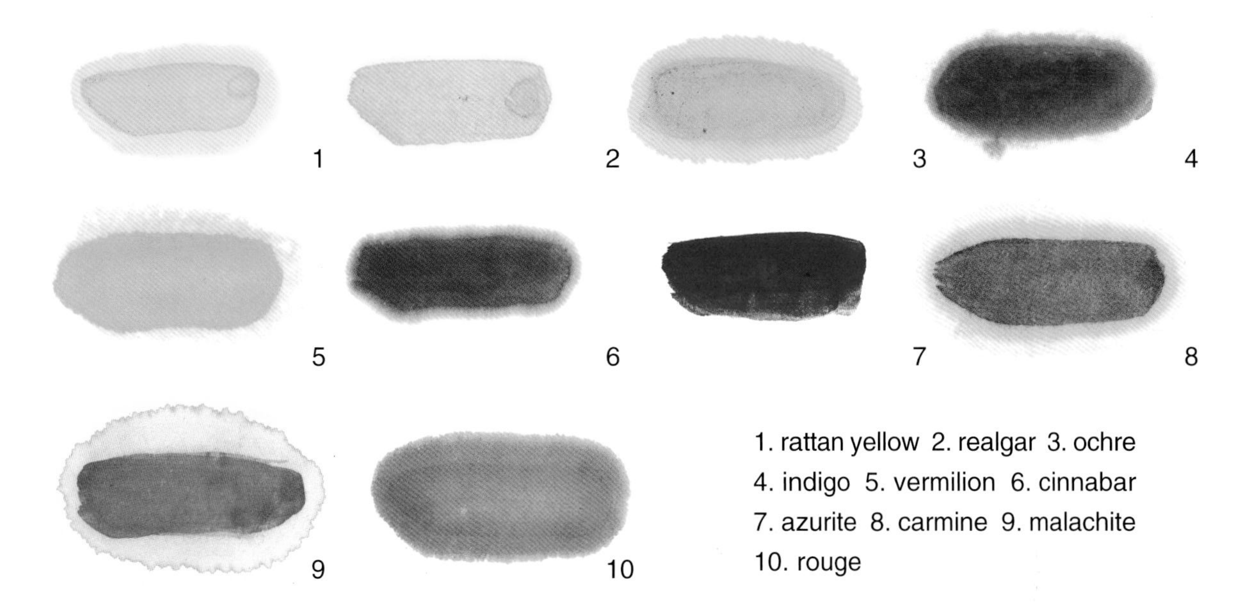

1. rattan yellow 2. realgar 3. ochre
4. indigo 5. vermilion 6. cinnabar
7. azurite 8. carmine 9. malachite
10. rouge

you should never let it touch your mouth. Dissolve it with cold water as in hot water it will become drossy. You can also grind the caked rattan yellow against an ink stone when the newly ground colour will be brilliant. When soaked in water for a long time, it will become dark. This can be mixed with ink, red or ochre.

Rouge (*yanzhi* 胭脂). Usually in cakes or flakes, it is dissolved in clean water. It is used for underpainting. It can be mixed with ink, vermilion or ochre.

Ochre (*zheshi* 赭石). This comes as glued powder which should be mixed with clear water. It is used in underpainting or for colouring tree-trunks. Though a mineral colour, it is rather transparent. It is used by itself or can be mixed with ink, indigo or green. When mixing ochre with other colours, don't stir the colours too much, or the mixture will become muddy.

Malachite (*shilü* 石绿[緑]). It comes in powder or in sticks. A malachite stick can be ground on a stone (you will need a separate stone for colours), and the powder must be used with glue. It is usually produced in four shades, in a descending order of darkness: the malachite label one, label two, label three and label four (*toulü, erlü, sanlü, silü* 头[頭]绿，二绿，三绿，四绿). Malachite is often used with the herbal green (mixture of indigo and rattan yellow) and ochre, with the herbal green and the ochre used as underpainting. Sometimes, malachite is also used as an underpainting colour to set off herbal green.

Azurite (*shiqing* 石青). The properties and use are similar to those of malachite. It is also graded to azurite label one, label two, label three and label four (*touqing, erqing, sanqing, siqing* 头[頭]青，二青，三青，四青), and is applied on a ground of indigo or carmine. This colour is applied in several layers. The new coating must be applied only when the first layer has become dry.

Carmine (*yanghong* 洋红). This is a cream that can be dissolved in water. Nowadays its substitute in a tube is used. It is used to depict peach blossom, lotus and peony. In landscape it is used in underpainting. You can obtain a purple by mixing it with indigo.

Cinnabar (*zhusha* 朱砂). It comes in sticks or in powder form. The powder must be mixed with glue and is used the same way as malachite and azurite. It is applied on a ground of ink or rouge. Do not mix it with vegetable colours like indigo, rattan yellow or scarlet. Avoid mixing with malachite or azurite or you will get a smudgy grey.

Vermillion (*zhubiao* 朱膘). This colour comes in glued cakes or flakes and is dissolved in clear water. It is a stone colour, but like ochre, is usually mixed with rouge, scarlet, rattan yellow and other vegetable colours. When mixed with ink, it is a bright brown colour that does not hinder the smooth movement of the brush.

Tube colours available in the market today are chemicals. They are handy but they have different properties from those of traditional Chinese colours. For example, tube colour rattan yellow can cover the underlayer of colour while the traditional rattan yellow is transparent.

Tube colours

rattan yellow (gamboge) | ochre (burnt sienna) | vermillion | cinnabar | scarlet

rouge | indigo | azurite | phthalocynine blue | malachite

Illustration by Wen Jingen

The cinnabar in tube is not as bright as the traditional cinnabar. The indigo in tube is dazzling while the indigo powder is calm. The ochre in tube is smudgy if it is in strong shade and it is yellowish when used in light shade. The ochre powder is fine and pure.

	rattan yellow	ochre	cinnabar	indigo
traditional colour				
tube colour				

Comparison of traditional Chinese colours and tube colours (illustration by Wen Jingen)

Accessories

Besides the four rudimentary tools, some accessories are indispensable. If you paint on unsized paper (most paintings in this book are done on unsized paper), you need a piece of **painting felt** (not craft felt). Put the felt under your paper when you paint, otherwise the ink and colour will run through your paper, wet the table, come back into your paper and smudge.

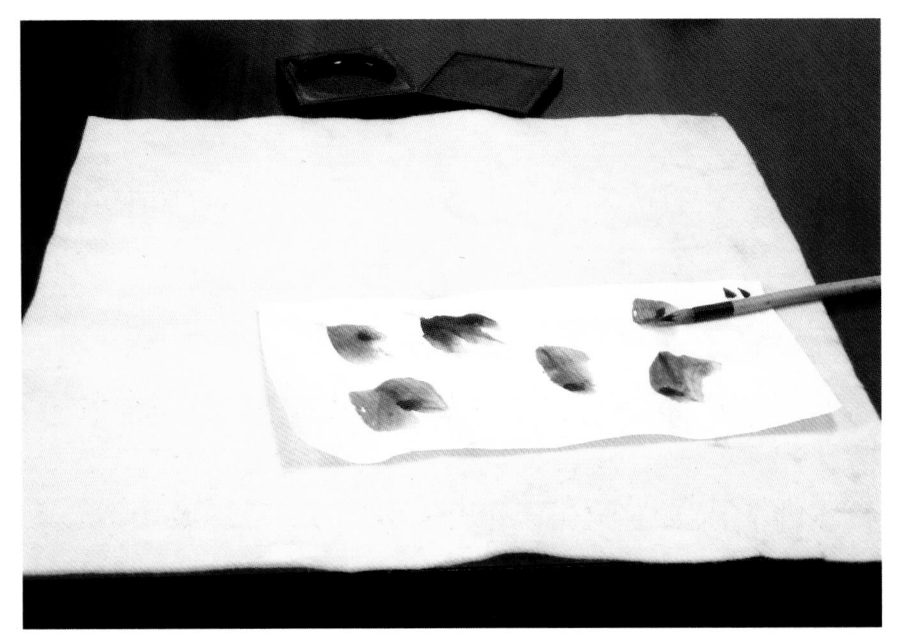

Illustration by Wen Jingen

You need a bowl to wash your brushes. The **palette** used by Chinese painters is made of porcelain. Many painters use separate dishes instead of a palette especially when producing a large painting.

Many Chinese painters like to impress their seals on their paintings. These can be a name seal, a studio seal or a message seals. You can carve your own or go to a professional seal carver. Needless to say, you will need seal paste too.

Photograph by Sun Shuming

A **brush roll**, usually made from split bamboo, protects your brushes when you travel.

Photograph by Sun Shuming

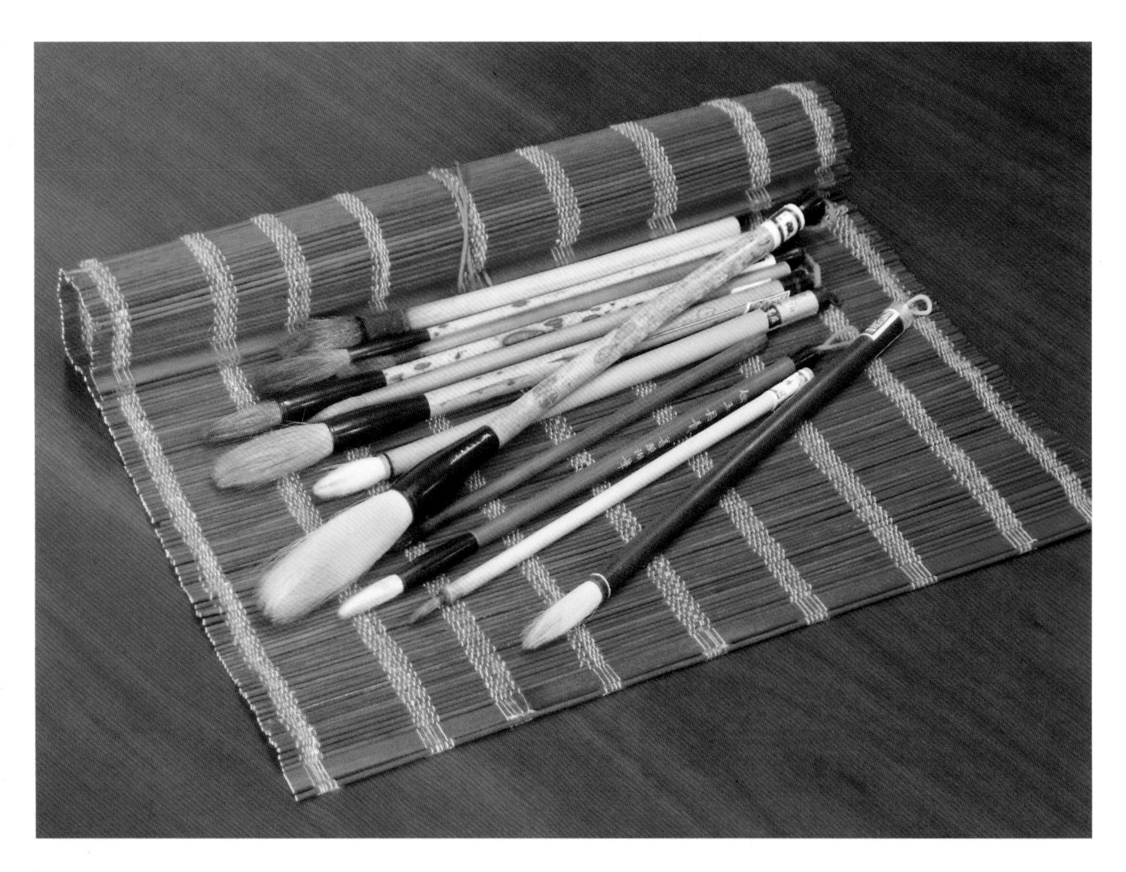

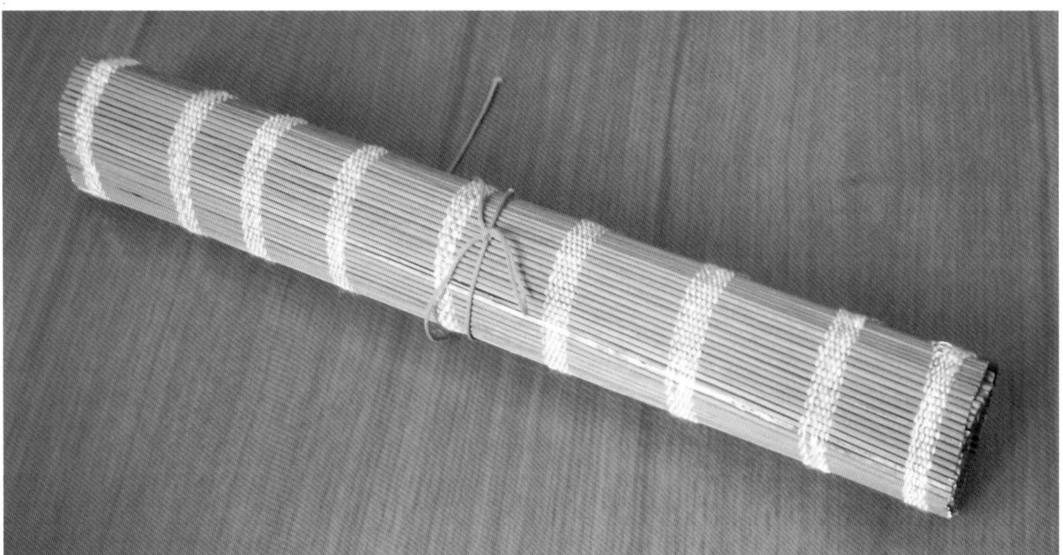

Illustrations by Wen Jingen

The Brush and Strokes

Hold the brush with your thumb and all your fingers. When you paint a line, all your fingers should work in coordination. The thumb, forefinger and middle finger hold the brush shaft, the ring finger pushes the brush shaft outwards and the little finger reinforces the ring finger.

Today nearly all Chinese calligraphers stress that the brush must be held vertically. But I recommend that the brush be kept in an 80-degree angle with the paper. This will help you keep the brush tip at the centre of the stroke it produces. A stroke produced this way is called "centre-tip" stroke (*zhongfeng* 中锋[鋒]).

A stroke produced by keeping the brush tip at one side of the stroke is called "side-tip stroke" (*cefeng* 侧锋[側鋒]). In doing a side-tip stroke, the brush shaft is usually held at a slant. Sometimes even the root of the brush touches the paper to produce rough, ragged marks. Such strokes play an important role in landscape.

Illustration by Wen Jingen

The brush tip may leave its trace at the end of a stroke, or be concealed in the stroke.

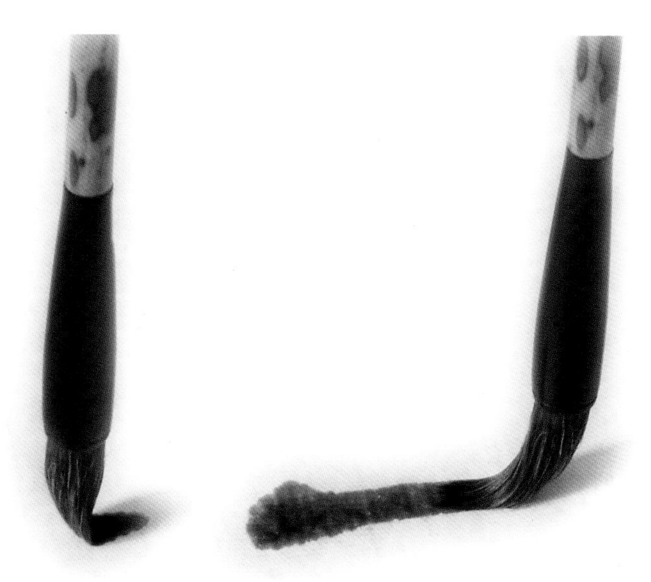

Start a stroke by moving the brush tip to the left a little

Turn the brush tip to the right and move it

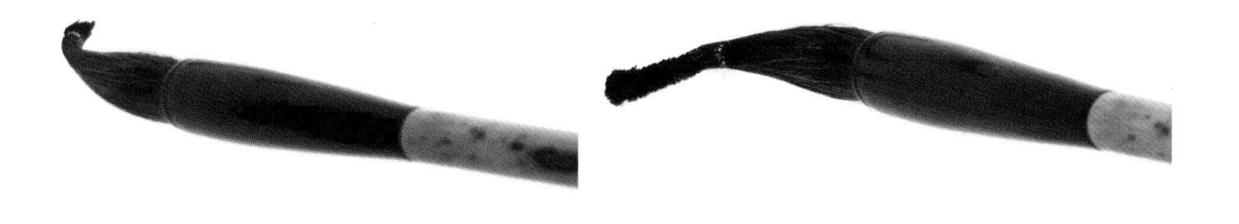

Begin a stroke by moving the brush to the left slightly

Turn the brush tip and move it to the right

End the stroke and turn the brush tip back

Turn the brush tip leftward and finish the stroke

Result: a stroke with the trace of the brush tip concealed at its both ends

Begin a dot by moving the brush upward slightly

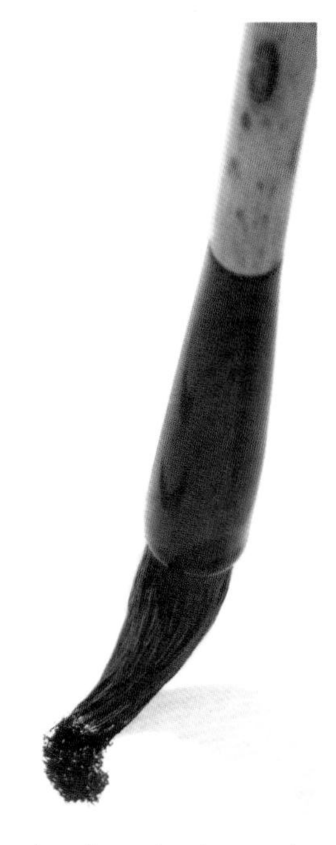

Turn the brush tip and move it downward and leftward

Move the brush tip to the right

Result: a round dot

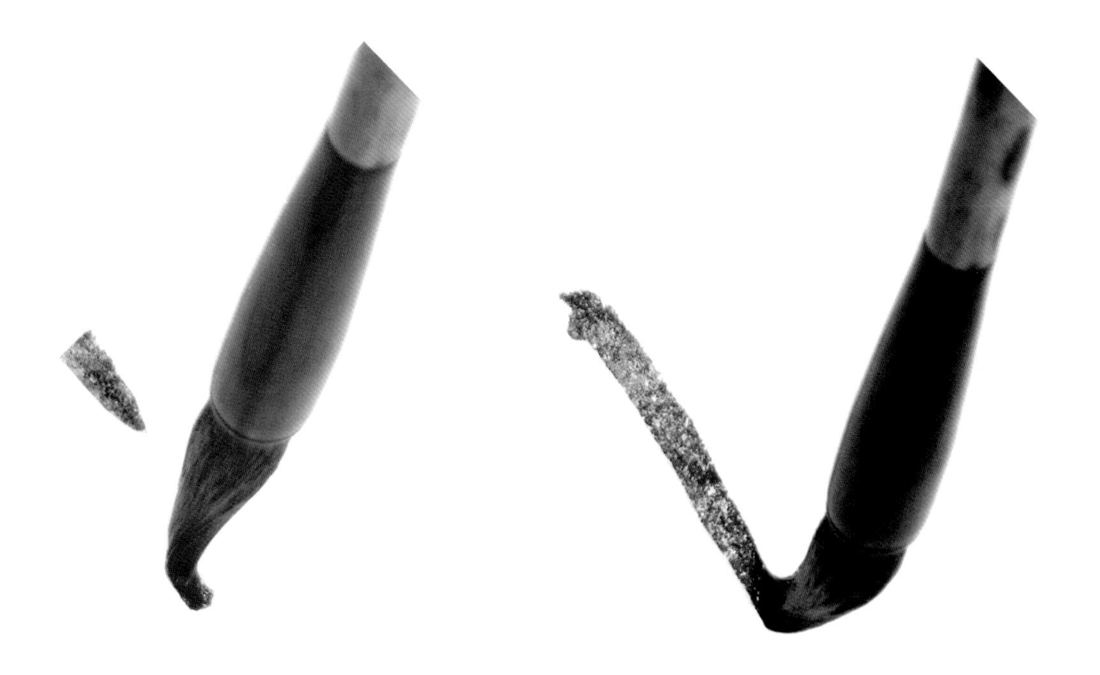

Begin a stroke by moving the brush upward slightly

Turn the brush and move it downward

End the brush by lifting the brush from paper

Result: a stroke with the trace of brush tip concealed at one end

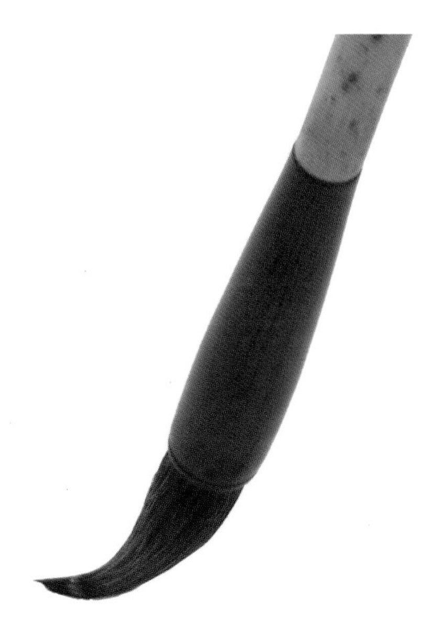

Begin a stroke directly

Move the brush

Lift the brush from paper

Result: a stroke with the trace of the brush tip exposed at both ends

The brush may be moved in forward or reverse directions: i.e., you can "pull" the brush along or "push" it against the direction of the tip. The turning of a stroke may be round or angular.

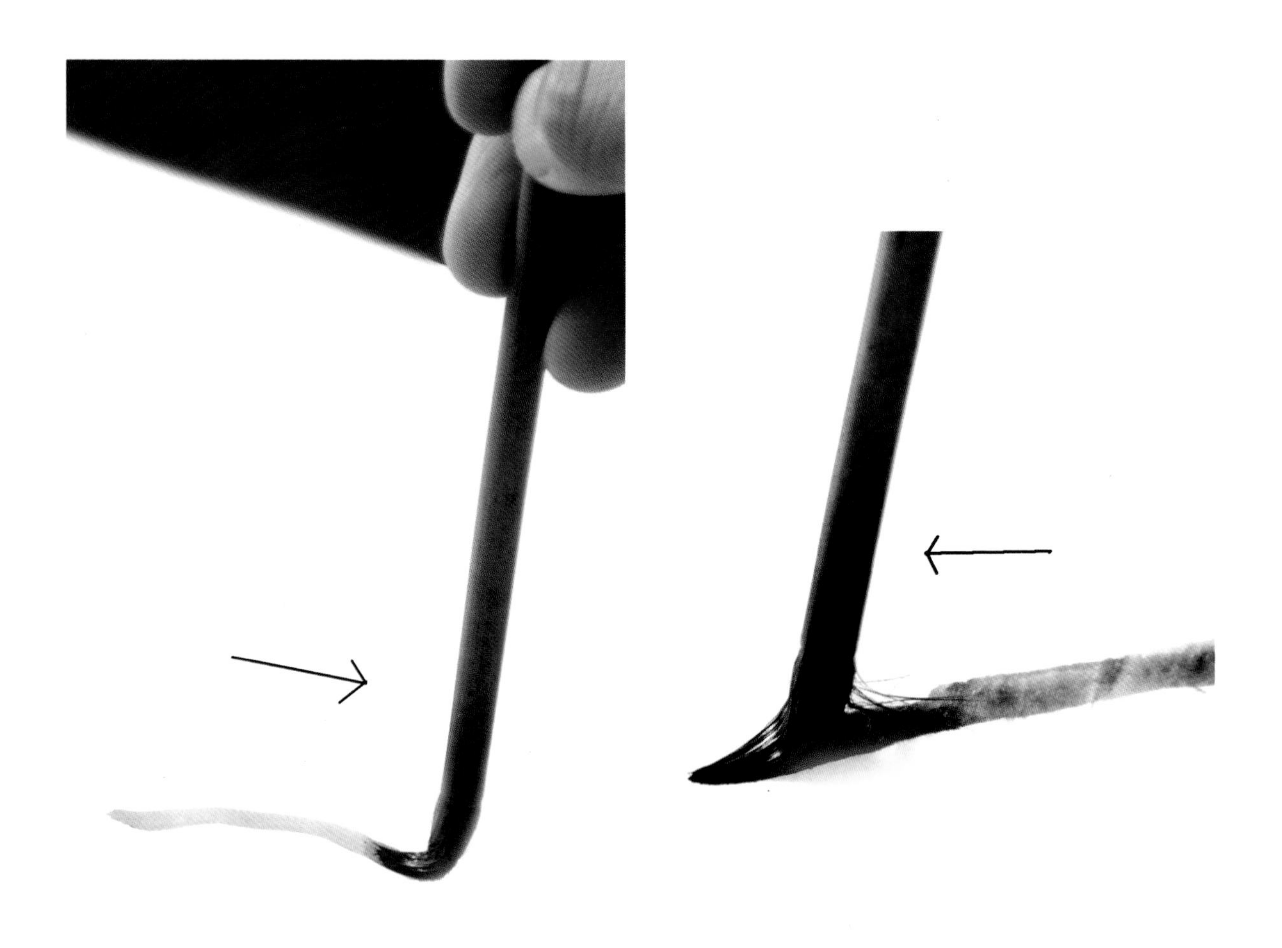

pulling stroke

pushing stroke

Illustrations by Wen Jingen

Sometimes you will need to press your brush down onto the paper or raise it from the paper, thus making part of your stroke different from others.

The fibres in the brush should generally be kept adjacent to each other to form a good point, but for a particular effect the fibres may be made to spread loosely. Strokes executed by spreading fibres often serve special purposes.

Illustration by Wen Jingen

Building structure through brushwork 骨法用笔(筆) is the second of the "Six Canons" (*liu fa* 六法) put forward by the artist and art historian Xie He who was active around AD 500 (the other five being 1. presenting the bearing and vigour (of the depicted person); 3. depicting the forms of things as they are; 4. appropriate colouring; 5. composition; and 6. transcribing and copying). This "canon" makes the brushwork an important yardstick for judging the quality of a painting. These principles were originally written at a time when figure painting was predominant.

Control the brush but do not be controlled by the brush. 使笔(筆)不可反为(爲)笔(筆)使 Because the tip of a Chinese brush is much softer than that of an oil painting brush, a beginner may find it difficult to achieve desired strokes. It takes some time to learn to control the brush. If you do not exert yourself to the command of your brush but instead take any stroke your brush produces, you are at mercy of your brush and you will never achieve desired brushwork!

"Strength" in brushwork. Forceful strokes are appreciated in Chinese painting. The "strength" of brushwork does not mean a great physical effort. Instead, it is an outcome of a long training. When we view a painting of Peter Rubens, we are not only impressed by the beautiful images in the painting, but are fascinated with his powerful brushwork as well. Compare an original masterpiece in a museum with a copy on sale in a roadside shop and you will notice the difference between them: they bear like images, but the brushwork in the copy is much "weaker" than that in the original. Although a clear-cut definition of strong and weak brushwork is not available, as you view more Chinese paintings and compare different works, you will learn to discern the "strength" contained in brushwork, just as it is not difficult for you to tell the footprints of a firm and steady walker from those of a drunkard or one with a limp.

Powerful brushwork is achievable through practice. The key to success is always keeping in your mind the strokes you are aiming at and how you will achieve them (keeping the tip at the centre or one side of your stroke, pressing or raising the brush, moving the brush quickly or slowly, "pulling" or "pushing" your brush etc.).

Shades of ink. In Chinese painting ink plays a more important role than colour. A painting can be executed without colour but cannot be without ink. By adding water, ink can be diluted into different shades: dark, black, light or pale. The extreme dry ink is called dried-up ink (*jiaomo* 焦墨). This ink is produced by grinding an ink stick on an ink stone until the liquid is thick and dry. Bottled ink does not have this grade of darkness. So if you want to get dried-up ink using a bottled ink, you must put the ink into an ink stone and grind an ink stick into it.

Illustration by Wen Jingen

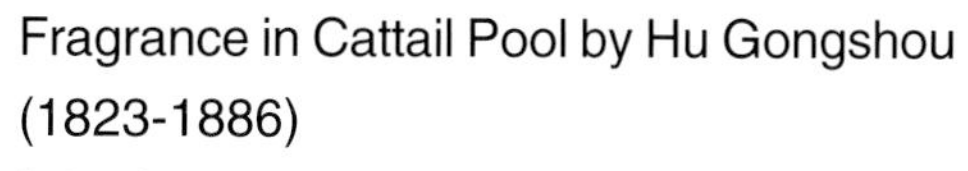

Fragrance in Cattail Pool by Hu Gongshou (1823-1886)
Ink plays a more important role than a black colour. In this painting green leaves are depicted in ink.

You can put further ink strokes on dry ink marks. This technique is called multilayer or accumulated ink (*jimo* 积[積]墨).

Rainy Landscape by Yu Gui,1846. Note the accumulated ink dots.

If you put ink strokes on wet ink, this technique is called wet-on-wet ink (*pòmo* 破墨).

Oversaturated brushwork is called splash-ink (*pōmo*泼[潑]墨). (Note: the Chinese for wet-on-wet is "pòmo", with "po" in falling tone and splash-ink, "pōmo", with "po" in flat tone. In Chinese language each syllable is tonal. In English a sylłable may be accented or unaccented.) Apart from splashing ink, you can also splash colour.

Wet-on-wet: colours
Wet-on-wet, Illustration by Wen Jingen

Splash-ink landscape
by Wen Jingen

You can splash colour too! (landscape by Wen Jingen)

Texture-stroke (*cun* 皴) and skimming stroke (*ca* 擦). Texture-strokes are made using repeated side-tip strokes in light ink to represent the surface of a rock or tree trunk. If the stroke is dry and loose so that the traces of brushwork are invisible, this is called a skimming stroke.

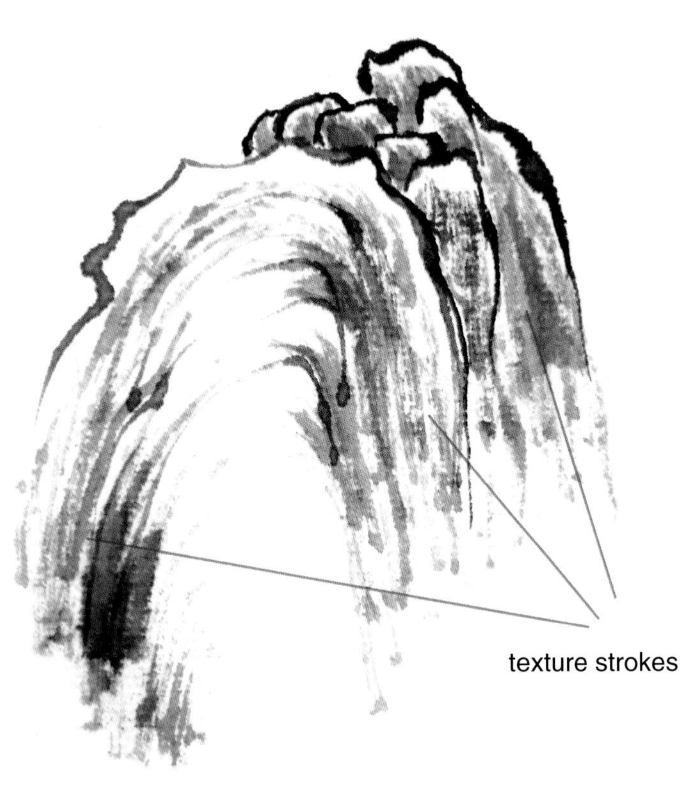

skimming strokes

Illustrations by Wen Jingen

Techniques of Painting Different Objects in Landscape

Trees

Ancient artists compared trees to the clothing of a mountain. A bare landscape is uninteresting and does not help the viewer to cultivate their aesthetic taste. Trees play a crucial part in a landscape.

You may begin with branches of a bare tree. According to the form of the branches, Chinese landscape painters put various trees into two categories: the antler (*lu jiao* 鹿角) and the crab's claw (*xie zhao* 蟹爪).

Four-stroke method. To get started, you may use the four-stroke method: The first stroke is right upward. This stroke determines the pose of a bough or a tree. The stroke is started with the brush-tip concealed with it. The second stroke goes downward and then up. The third stroke crosses the second stroke. The last stroke goes upwards. Repeat this to build up a tree.

"Antler" in four-stroke method

“Crab’s claw” in four-stroke method

Contracting boughs and spreading leaves. A tree consists of the root, the trunk, branches and leaves. The trunk and the treetop are the major parts. To make a pleasing tree, you may contract the branches and spread the canopy. A mushroom-shaped treetop is unattractive.

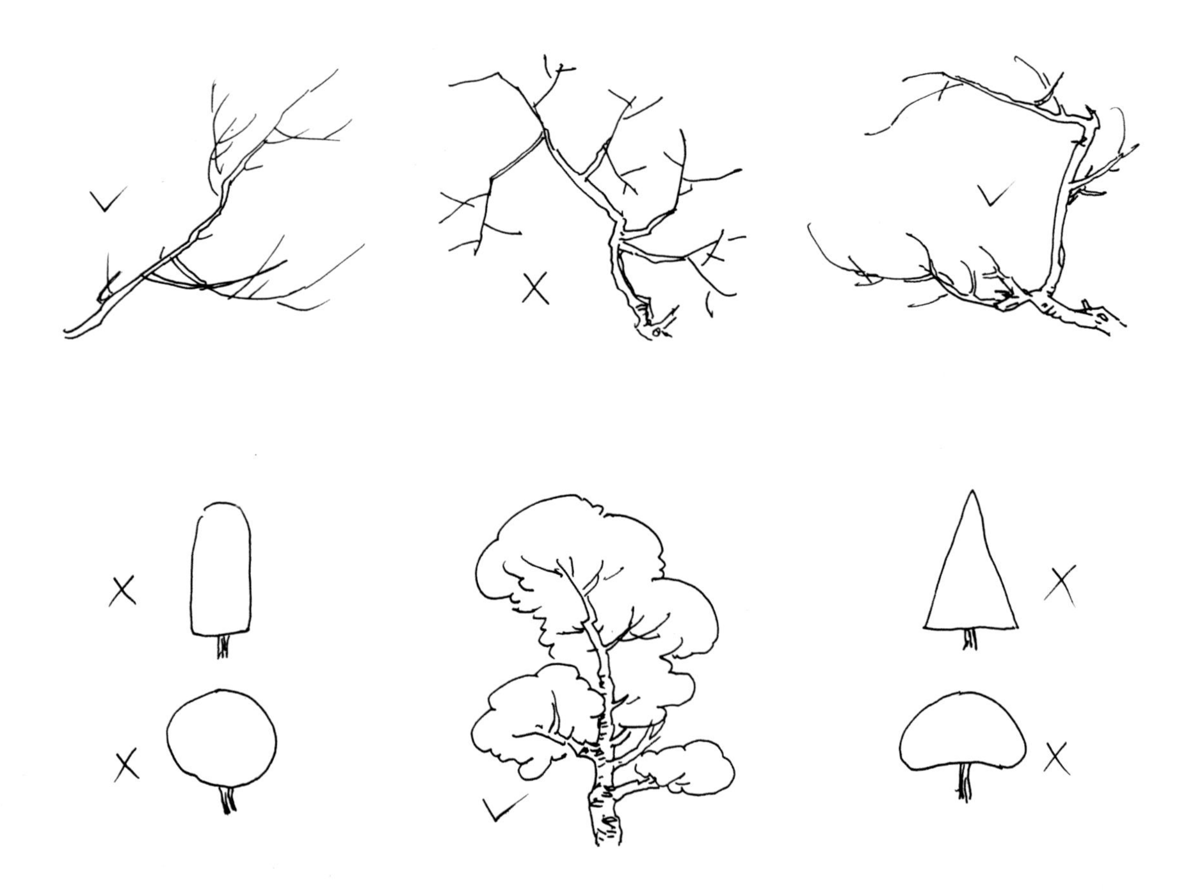

The top and side branches. Different trees have a variety of tops. The accurate depiction of the treetop helps to portray the features of different trees. This is especially important for trees in the background of a landscape painting. The side branches also set off the characteristics of the tree form and the landscape painter should display his or her masterly brushwork and ink skill in depicting the side branches.

Braving the wind. A side branch looks best when it is depicted as "braving the wind". In the face of a wind the branch appears vigorous. It grows towards a space where there is sufficient air and sunshine. The environment also determines a branch's growth. For example, a tree by a wall tends to extend its branches outward, and a tree by a stream tends to extend its branches towards the water surface. A downward branch always has its end upward. A rightward branch always has its end turning leftwards, and vice versa.

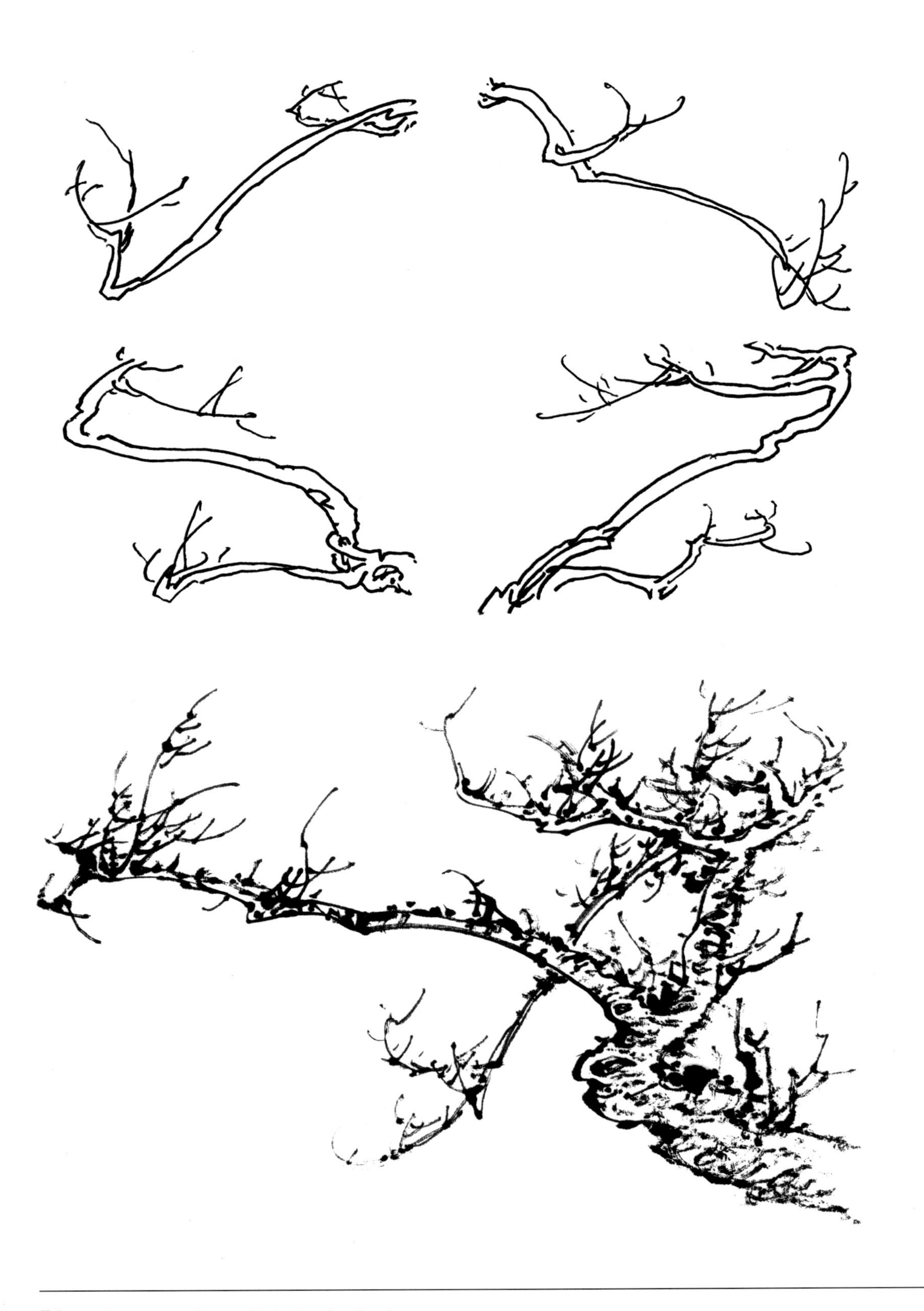

Leaves. Tree leaves can be outlined (*jiaye* 夹叶[夾葉]) or "dotted" with the brush (*dianye* 点叶[點葉]).

Uncontoured trees by Wen Jingen

Pine. There is an old saying about portraying a pine, "The trunk is scaled, the boughs bowed and leaves are needles." Begin with the forked places and add branches to build up the tree. Leaves are added when the boughs are finished. Leaves are grouped in clusters and should be in uneven layers. The

scales on the trunk are oval circles but the circles are not necessarily complete. The outline of the trunk is executed with centre-tip strokes. Old pines often have knots at their roots. Here is the picture of a famous pine in Huangshan Mountains in central China.

Cypress. The coniferous evergreen tree enjoys an extraordinarily long life. Most cypresses grow on high mountains in cold zones. Due to lack of water, the tree grows slowly and its trunk tends to turn and twist. Paint the twisting trunk with centre-tip strokes and depict its leaves with dots. This is a half withered two-thousand-year cypress.

Poplar. Depict the trunk with side-tip strokes and depict the leaves with side-tip dots.

Willow. Willows often grow by rivers or pools. The trunk is depicted with slanting, short, centre-tip texture-strokes. The treetop is painted in sparse and terse lines. Leaves may be added as dots or coloured with broad ink marks.

Peach and pear trees. Peach trees usually grow on mounds with short trunk and boughs. In landscape paintings pink peach blossom imbues the painting with splendour of springtime. It often appears in juxtaposition with white pear blossom.

China fir. An evergreen tree growing in sunny and damp regions along the Yangzi River, the China fir has straight veins on its bark and its leaves look like hanging needles, which are usually depicted with centre-tip long dots. The top is in the shape of umbrella spokes.

Wingceltis (Sandalwood). This hardwood tree grows slowly. A species of this tree on Mount Cangyan in the Taihang Mountains has a grotesque trunk with thick leaves and a root which winds into rock cracks. The root is larger than the trunk.

Chinese wisteria and vines. Perennial tropical plants which cling to and smother other plants, especially to old trees in landscape paintings.

Rocks and Texture-strokes

Different texture-strokes show the veins, structure, volume, or light and shade of rocks as seen in a distance. Dozens of texture-strokes fall into two categories, the hemp-fibre strokes (*pima cun* 披麻皴) and the axe-cut strokes (*fupi cun* 斧劈皴).

Hemp-fibre strokes. Contour rocks with centre-tip strokes in light ink, and repeatedly shade the dark places with texture-strokes. When the rocks are well modelled, add dots to them. Rocks depicted in this kind of texture look round and smooth.

Step 1. Outline rocks with centre-tip strokes. Usually the brush is "pulled" along the contour of rocks. The few initial lines not only represent the contour of rocks, but their grain, volume, structure and tactile value. In the Western drawing the line usually presents the contour of an object. Line in Chinese painting presents more than the contour stroke — these lines should be lively and animated. Dull strokes should be avoided.

- The first stroke is made by concealing the brush tip in the stroke, turn the brush and end the line with the trace of the brush tip exposed.
- The second stroke is added under the first stroke.
- The third stroke continues the first stroke.
- The fourth stroke goes downwards and turns at the bottom.
- The fifth stroke is zigzagging and extends outward.

Step 2. Adding texture-strokes. Like hatching in drawing, texture-strokes help to show the volume of depicted objects. The hemp-fibre strokes are centre-tip marks added within the contour and along the vein and structure of the rocks. Texture-strokes also accentuate the perspective relationship among objects. Don't cross the texture-strokes and contour. Ink strokes should be in different shades.

Step 3. Shading with light ink washes. This step will put nuances into the depicted objects. Usually the top of a rock is lighter than its bottom; one side is lighter than the other. The tone on dense marks is darker than the tone on sparse strokes. After shading, the depicted objects look simpler and fuller.

Step 4. Adding dots. This is the final step. Use a blunt stiff-fibre brush to add dots along the contour or veins of rocks. The dots should not be added evenly — some places should have more dots than others. The dots should be round and full — so do not use a new brush or goat-fibre brush, for they tend to produce limp dots.

Loosened strands stroke *jiesuo cun* 解索皴. A variety of the hemp-fibre stroke, this looks like a hemp rope with its strands loosened, dangling and twisting. Usually the contour and texture-strokes on the top of rocks is darker than those at the bottom. Sometimes these kind of strokes are used in combination with the hemp-fibre strokes, hence the name "hemp-fibre-loosened-strands" strokes.

Lotus-leaf stroke *heye cun* 荷叶(葉)皴. This kind of stroke shows the grain of rocks in lines grouped in form of the veins of a lotus leaf. The beginning of such a stroke is darker and broader than its end. It is used to depict towering mountains, mounds and traces left by scouring floods.

Cloud stroke *yuntou cun* 云头(雲頭)皴. This stroke is employed to depict certain igneous rocks. This stroke is a round and turning centre-tip stroke.

Illustration by Wen Jingen

Disordered firewood stroke *luanchai cun* 乱(亂)柴皴. This kind of brushwork is used to depict rocks in shapes of disordered firewood or a mass of hemp. The brushwork is free but not careless. Usually the stroke is started with a centre-tip stroke and ended with tip fibre loosely spread. The brush may rotate when this kind of stroke is applied. Quick and slow movement of the brush, combined with dark and light ink shades, make this brushwork varied and expressive. It can be used to depict mountains covered with shrubs.

Axe-cut stroke. This stroke is used to depict hard rocks and cliffs. First contour rocks with centre-tip strokes, and add texture-strokes with a side-tip brush. The turnings in these strokes should be angular so as to fit the edges of the depicted rocks, but out of place edges should be avoided. Variants of this stroke include horse-tooth stroke, raindrop stroke, bending tape stroke and "slurry" stroke.

Texture-strokes of this type must leave a gap between the outline and lines used to indicate the structure, so as to keep a space to suggest reflection of light on the edge of the dark surface.

Horse-tooth stroke *maya cun* 马(馬)牙皴. This is derived from the axe-cut stroke. Use a small brush than that used for axe-cut stroke, and add square strokes with side-tip brushwork.

Rain-drop stroke *yudian cun* 雨点(點)皴. This stroke is produced with side-tip brushwork. The strokes are small dots like raindrops, hence the name. If the strokes are smaller and denser, they are named sesame strokes (*zhima cun* 芝麻皴), and if the strokes are a bit longer, they become ox-hair strokes (*niumao cun* 牛毛皴).

Bending tape stroke *zhedai cun* 折带皴. This kind of stroke is used to depict horizontal layers of rocks. Apply this stroke with centre-tip brushwork and add side-tip strokes in light ink. It is used to depict high crags.

Slurry (Mud-and-water) stroke *tuo ni dai shui cun* 拖泥带水皴. This kind of texture-stroke is used in free style and splash-ink landscapes. Touch the paper with the point, middle part and the heel of a large brush, rotating the brush shaft. The result is a coherence of wet and dry marks in different shades. Avoid repeated strokes lest they become blurred and messy.

The names of the strokes are not as important as your close observation of nature. To present your objects more truthfully, you may use the named strokes but you may also create your own texture strokes.

Painting a stone: steps
(one of the many ways)

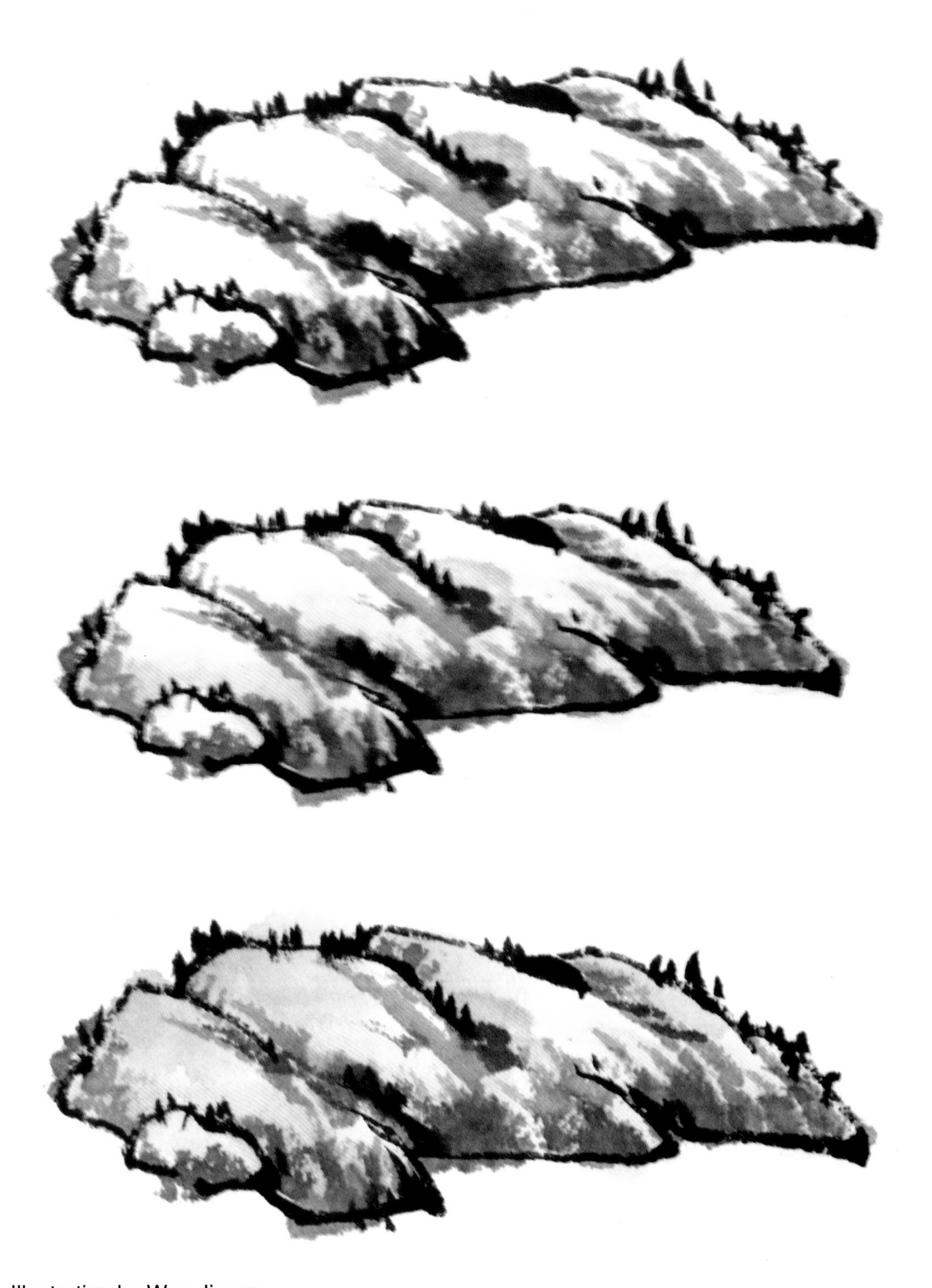

Illustration by Wen Jingen

Clouds and Water

As Chinese landscape is called "mountain-and-water" painting it suggests mountains and waters play a dominant role in this genre. Ancient Chinese say a waterfall is the blood of a mountain — with water flowing among rocks, the mountain is full of life.

Water may zigzag down towering peaks and form streams, passing through rocky clefts. At the foot of a mountain, water often runs into a lively brook. On the plain, these water torrents flow into rivers and maybe on into lakes. Water in an open sea can surge up to form huge waves.

Water has no definite shape, like a person's facial expression. Ancient Chinese artists used to depict water with lines and their painting vividly represented the spirit of water. Nowadays, Chinese artists have inherited this tradition and at the same time have developed new techniques. Many Chinese painters no more outline cloud and water. Instead they present cloud by leaving blank spaces amongst mountains that are depicted in ink and show water by leaving blank spaces against rocks that are depicted in dark ink.

We will study methods to depict waterfalls, cascades, streams and waves.

Waterfall. A waterfall is a string of water falling down from rocks or a cliff. It is depicted in two steps:

Step 1. Outline large and small rocks; paint the water with side-tip strokes from top to bottom (the top be darker than the lower part) and finally paint the rocks on each side of the water flow.

Step 2. Adding finishing touches. Show the details of rocks — the blank spaces among rocks show where the water flows. Further elaborate on the rocks. Usually the bottom of a rock is flat, do not let rocks run into each other. Show more details of the water and finally shade with ink. Thus the ink version of a waterfall is complete.

Cascades flowing down three terraces. At each terrace these are depicted in the same way. Attention must be given to the rocks in the foreground which should be in different sizes. The middle level of rocks should be in the form of stairs and the water flow should be long. The background has fewer rocks than the foreground and the middle section of the painting. The water flows should be depicted in light ink and colours. The mountains are steep in the foreground and become gentler on the background.

Waterfalls. Ancient artists say, "The waterfall is the bone of a mountain". The water is fluid, but it is powerful enough to rush through rocks. A good painting of a waterfall manifests the strenuous energy of water even though at places the flow is covered or not even depicted.

Clouds crossing waterfalls. In this painting the waterfalls from the top of the mountains are horizontally crossed by clouds. The clouds are not outlined but instead are shaded with light ink or colour. The water in the foreground is set off with bare rocks.

Water forking at a mountain pass. A waterfall may fork at its source. Usually a few streams join each other deep in the mountains. Sometimes part of the stream is covered by trees.

Finished version of the waterfalls after colour has been added to the painting

Hanging spring on a high cliff

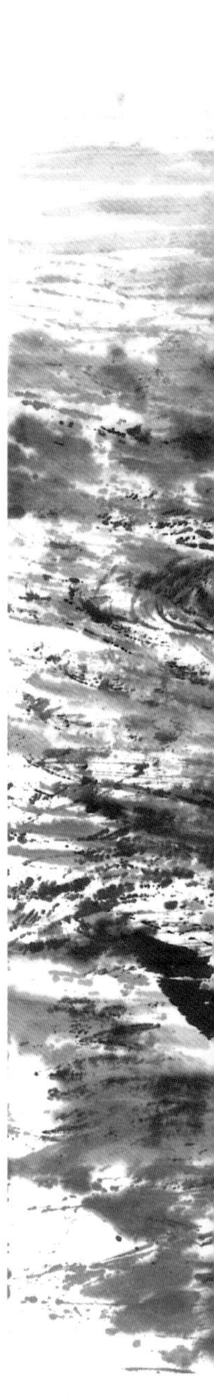

Expanse of waters. Waters may extend over a lake or sea. The calm water in moonlight and veiled in clouds makes a tranquil world.

Wave. Waves rise in windy weather. So the painting of waves is also the depiction of wind. Waves may be painted in line or shaded with ink and colour.

Cloud. Ancient artists thought that cloud was better shown by shading with ink and light colour. Even today most painters illustrate clouds by leaving unpainted spaces on the paper. In shading clouds, you should not go into too much detail. Outlined clouds often appear to be floating in wind.

In blue-and-green landscape paintings, clouds are usually outlined in light ink.

The impact of man

While buildings may become the main focus of a landscape painting in the West, in traditional Chinese "mountain-and-water" paintings, buildings and human figures usually serve as minor motifs strewn among mountains or by waters. But in a sense, such minor matters usually give highlight to a painting's theme. So they are still important. Here are some examples.

Houses

Bridges

wooden bridges, stone bridges

Boats

Humans

Birds and beasts

Painting a peak: steps:
(one of the many ways)

Illustration by Wen Jingen

Colouring

Chinese artists use local colours. A local colour is free from the influence of light and shade. However, this colour is not copied from nature. Instead, it is a bold subjective reflection based on the artist's individual perception. Ink plays the predominant part and colours work in concert with the ink. The colours should not conceal the ink; nor should the ink disturb the colours. The enchanting skills of brushwork and ink application make the colour in Chinese painting splendid, graceful and simple all at the same time.

A Chinese landscape painting may be in one of the three tones: light red, blue-and-green and golden-and-green. All of them are coloured using similar procedures:

1. Apply ink before colour. Light colouration is only applied when rocks, trees, houses, boats and other objects have been depicted in ink and the ink painting is complete.

2. Paint trees before rocks. Landscape accessories are coloured last.

3. Apply warm colours (red, ochre, orange, yellow, etc.) before cool colours (blue, green, etc.). Apply ochre before indigo and green.

4. Apply vegetable colours layer after layer. If the colour is not dark enough, add another layer. Repeat this procedure until the colour is in the right tone.

5. Apply the last coating at one go. The final coating of stone colour (azurite, malachite or cinnabar) should be applied only once.

6. At the final stage, dots in stone colours are added on treetops and rocks in the painting.

Light red landscape *(qianjiang shanshui* 浅绛[淺絳]山水). Also known as ink-and-wash landscape. This type of landscape, simple and graceful yet realistic, is executed mainly with ink, plus a little ochre and indigo. The colouring procedure is:

1. Apply ink first.

2. Apply vegetable colours repeatedly until the desired tone is achieved; always put new layers when the former coating has become dry.

3. The light sides of rocks are painted with ochre and the dark sides are coloured with indigo.

4. Tree trunks and boughs are shown with light ochre.

5. The leaves are painted with green or indigo. Usually the trees should be in stronger tone than mountains.

Stones in light red landscape can be coloured in four ways (in all cases colours are added after the ink marks are finished and dry):

1. add colour to the light side with ochre or ochre mixed with ink;

2. add colour to the dark side with ochre; when the colour is dry, add ochre mixed with ink;

3. paint and colour the light side with ochre and the dark side with ink mixed with ochre; or

4. add colour to the light side with ochre and colour the dark side with indigo.

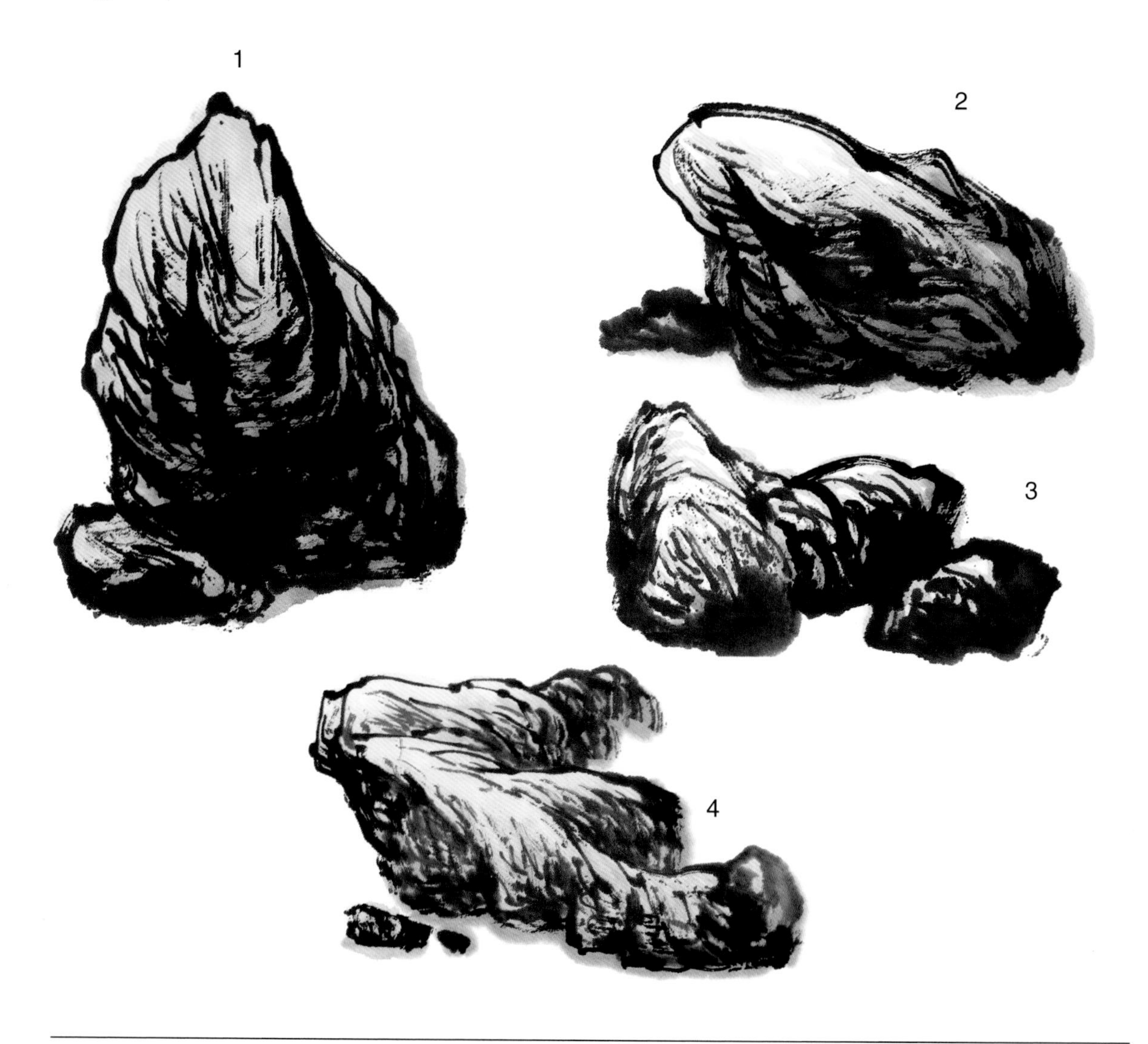

Blue-and-green landscape (*qinglü shanshui* 青绿[緑]山水). There are two subgenera: the lesser blue-and-green landscape and greater blue-and-green landscape.

The lesser blue-and-green landscape is a development of the light red landscape, adding malachite shades over the herbal green and thus enforcing the overall tone of green. To set off the green, the bare rock cliffs and beaches are coloured with ochre.

Step 2. covering the whole stone with malachite.

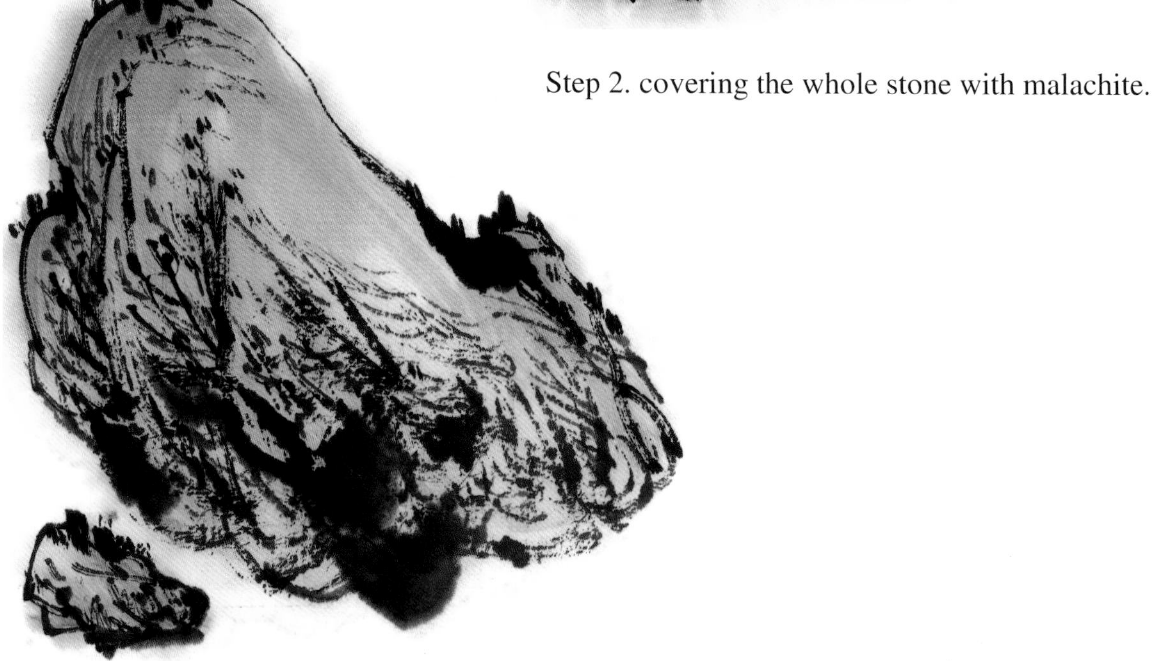

Step 1. colouring with transparent colour

Greater blue-and-green landscape is quite different from the lesser blue-and-green landscape.

To add colour to this type of landscape —

- paint the background with vegetable colours
- apply mineral colours
- finally, re-contour stones with colour lines. Colour dots are added at this stage.

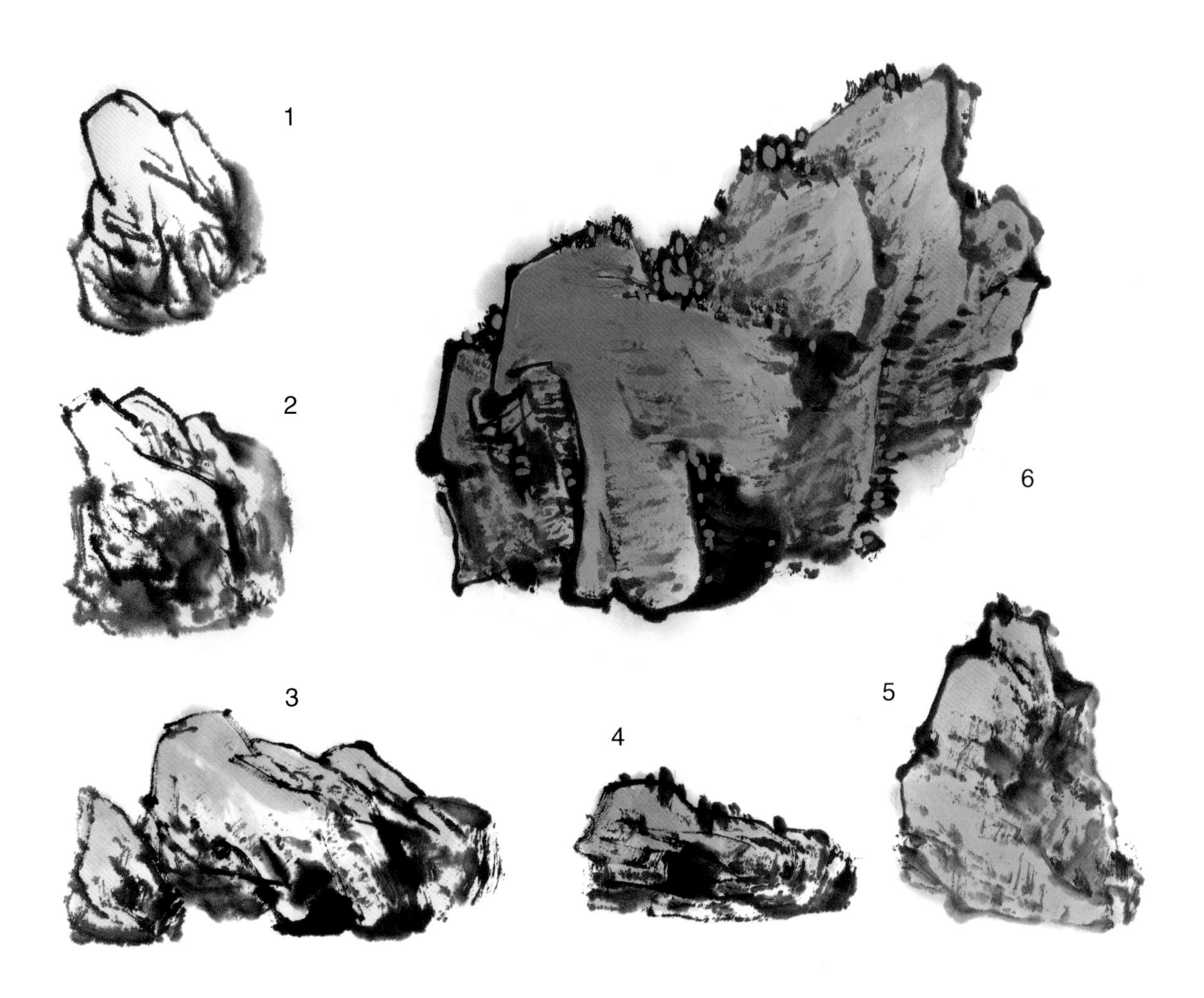

Great blue-and-green landscape, colour stronger than the lesser one

Uncontoured blue-and-green landscape by Liu Du (17th century)

The earliest extent blue-and-green landscape. This painting, attributed to the 8th-century blue-and-green landscape master Li Zhaodao, displays the emperor with his retinue fleeing away from the capital city to Sichuan region. The emperor had wallowed in debauchery, neglected state affairs and pampered his concubine in every way. He made her brother the Prime Minister who immediately arrogated all power to himself and the government was therefore in a bad shape. As a result, local warlords rose up in arms against the central government and took over the capital city. The emperor hurriedly fled from the city, and soon afterwards the soldiers in pursuit forced him to kill his concubine. It is extremely funny that the emperor and his followers in this painting look composed and at ease, as if they were on an excursion instead of an exile!

Gold-and-Green landscape *jinbi shanshui* 金碧山水. This splendid and grand subgenus is rather decorative. It is executed the same way as the greater blue-and-green landscape, but in the last procedure, the outlines and strata of the rocks are painted with golden lines. Note that a gold-and-green landscape is usually painted on sized silk or paper.

Clouds are contoured in white. Rocks and cliffs are coloured with thick layers of paint. The top of each rock is coloured with cool colour and the bottom of each is painted with warm colour — i.e., mountain tops are coloured with azurites, the middle part of mountains with malachite and the foot of mountains with ochre. Treetops are painted with indigo.

Pint flowers

Trees. Unlike trees in bird-and-flower painting, in landscapes they are coloured in accordance with the environment. Generally, tree trunks are painted with ochre. Leaves are coloured with indigo or herbal green (mixture of indigo and rattan yellow). Pink flowers (peach blossom) and white flowers (pear blossom) are both painted with white on different grounds. The ground for the former is crimson and that for the latter is herbal green. Roots of trees are not usually colour washed but have a secondary outline in light ochre.

Colouring trunks.

1. Add ochre to the ink strokes. When the ochre is dry, add ink mixed with ochre on both sides of the trunk so as to reinforce its volume value.

2, 3. Firs and cassia are coloured in the same way as the pine.

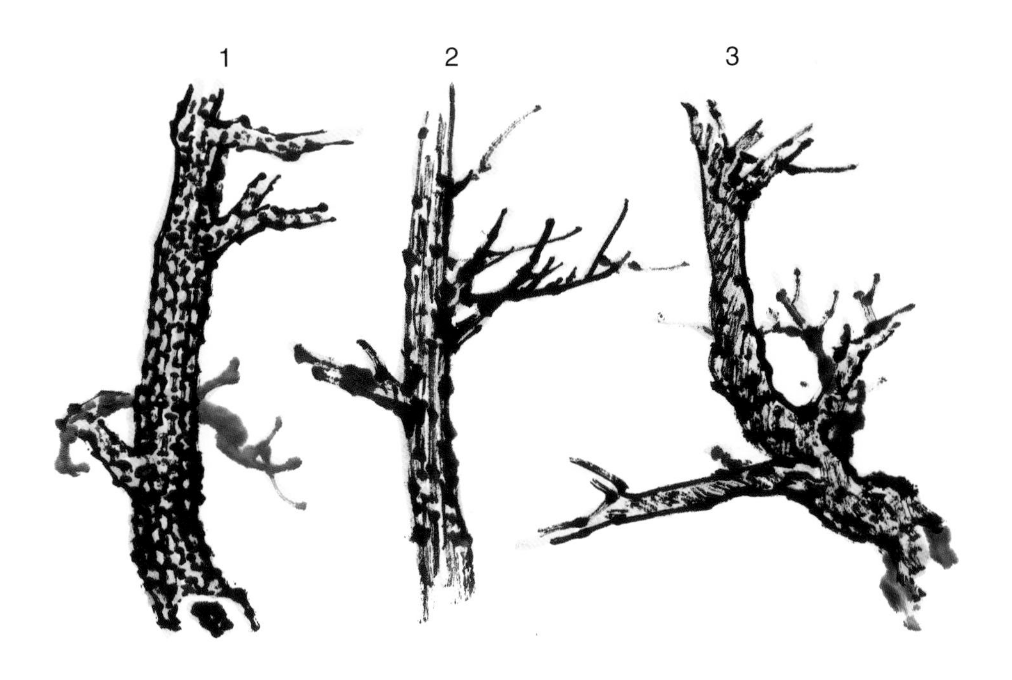

4. Some trunks are outlined. Just add ochre lines over the ink ones.

5. To colour branches executed in ink, ochre strokes can be added on top of the ink.

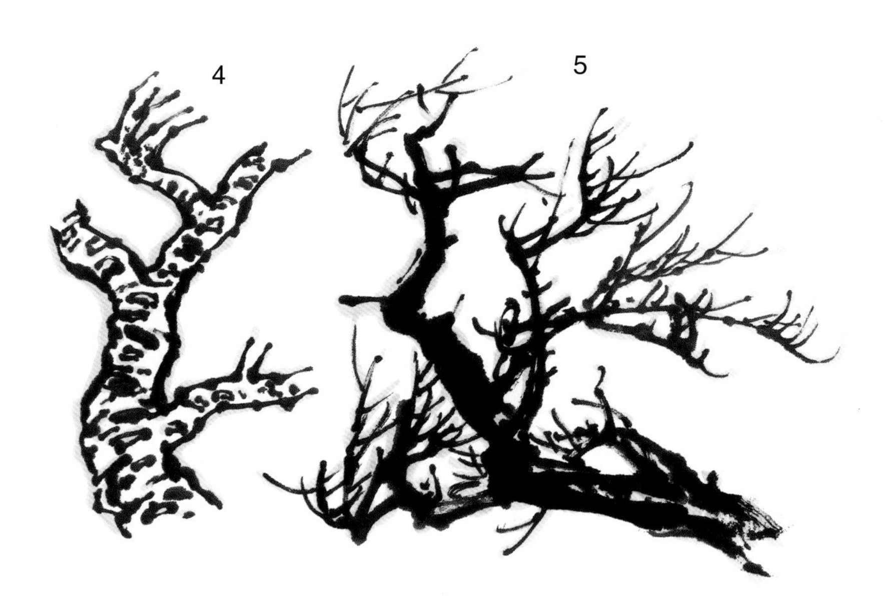

If leaves are outlined, apply a ground wash with indigo, herbal green, rouge, crimson or light ochre before filling in the outlines with azurites, malachites, cinnabar or mineral yellow.

Pines can be painted in ink and coloured with indigo (upper left). Azurite dots can be added to ink dots (upper second from the right). Willow branches can be coloured with herbal green (rattan yellow mixed with indigo) (upper right). Some outlined leaved may be coloured with herbal green and when the first layer of colour is dry, add malachite on the centre of each group of "petals" (lower left).

Frost-bitten red leaves can be painted using ink mixed with carmine. When the lines are dry, add dots of cinnabar. The trunks can be over-painted with ochre. Peach blossoms can be painted with carmine. When the carmine is dry, add dots in thick white.

The underpainting of dotted green leaves is black green or grey green. The underpainting of yellow leaves is ochre yellow or deep yellow.

Painting trees: steps

Contour trunks

Add dot and outlined leaves

Add colours
Illustrations by Wen Jingen

Painting landscape: steps

Draft with charcoal

Add ink dots and lines

Add more ink dots and texture strokes

Add azurite (or malachite) dots on ink marks, add ochre to rocks and indigo to distant peaks. Leave some places uncoloured.

Illustrations by Wen Jingen

Draft with charcoal

Outline peaks

Add texture strokes

Add ink dots

Illustrations by
Wen Jingen

Add azurite dots on ink marks, colour rocks with ochre

Painting from Life

Painting from life is a basic training for a Chinese painter. While a painter travels he or she observes the topographical features of rocks and mountains, the direction of the ridgelines and records these with a brush on his paper. This is in fact a procedure of creation that is quite different from copying a picture in the studio. To put what is seen onto paper, the artist has to use the brain. He or she has to convert a three-dimensional vision into two-dimensional images. On the other hand, to paint from life is not the same thing as capturing images with a camera. A painter must learn to discern, understand and choose the most essential and most typical features of what falls into his or her eyes. When painting from life, the artist applies what is learned from beginner's manuals to practice of painting.

Multi-focus perspective

To compose a painting, you must know something about perspective. In Western drawing and painting (oil painting, watercolour etc.) linear perspective is usually applied. Linear perspective is a geometric method of representing objects so that they appear three-dimensional.

Perspective theory applied in Western painting presumes that all side edges of an object placed flat recede to vanishing points on the horizon line. If you put a piece of glass vertically in front of your eyes and draw what you see through the glass, you will achieve a picture with correct perspective. Understandably, in doing this, you cannot turn your head left or right, up or down. You have a fixed "focus". Your picture displays what your field of vision holds, the same as a photograph of the scene.

Single-point perspective: all horizontal lines vanish at a point (S)

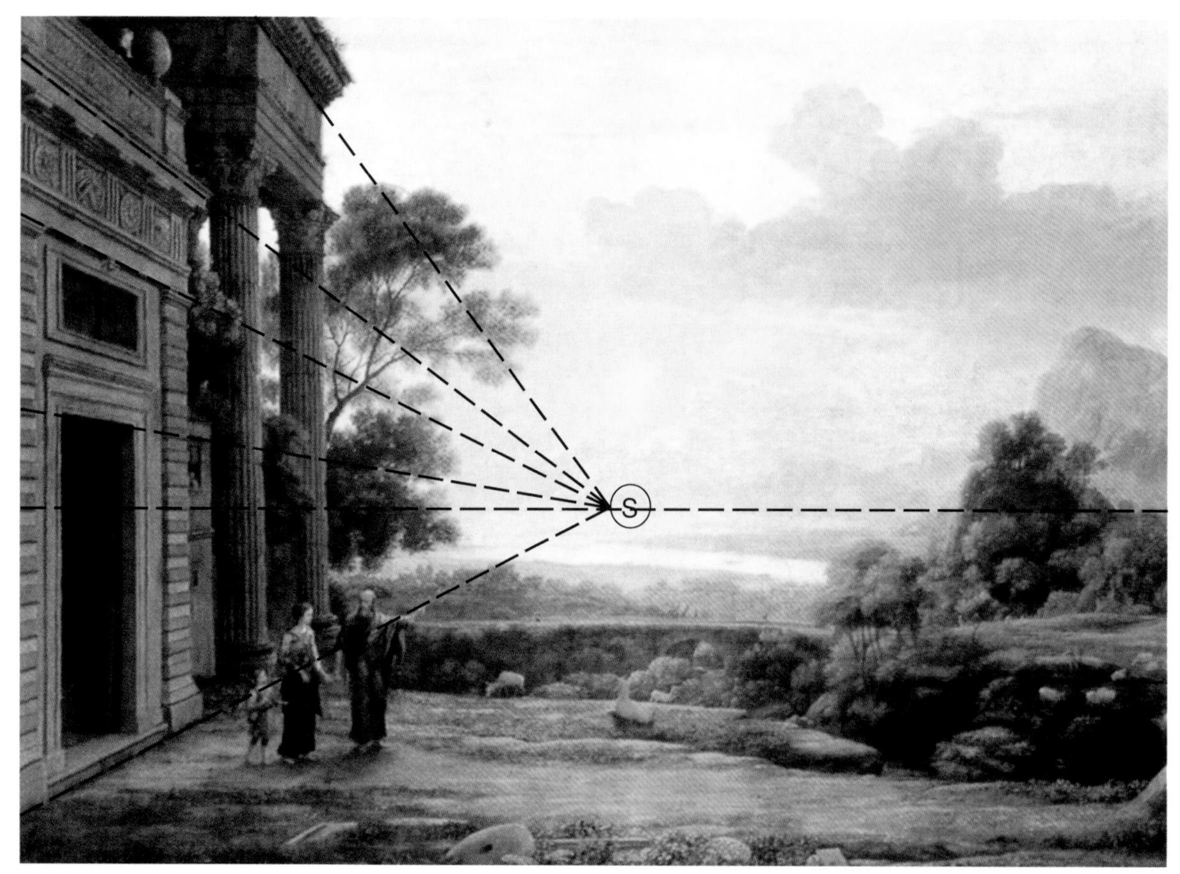

by Claude lorraine (1600-1682)

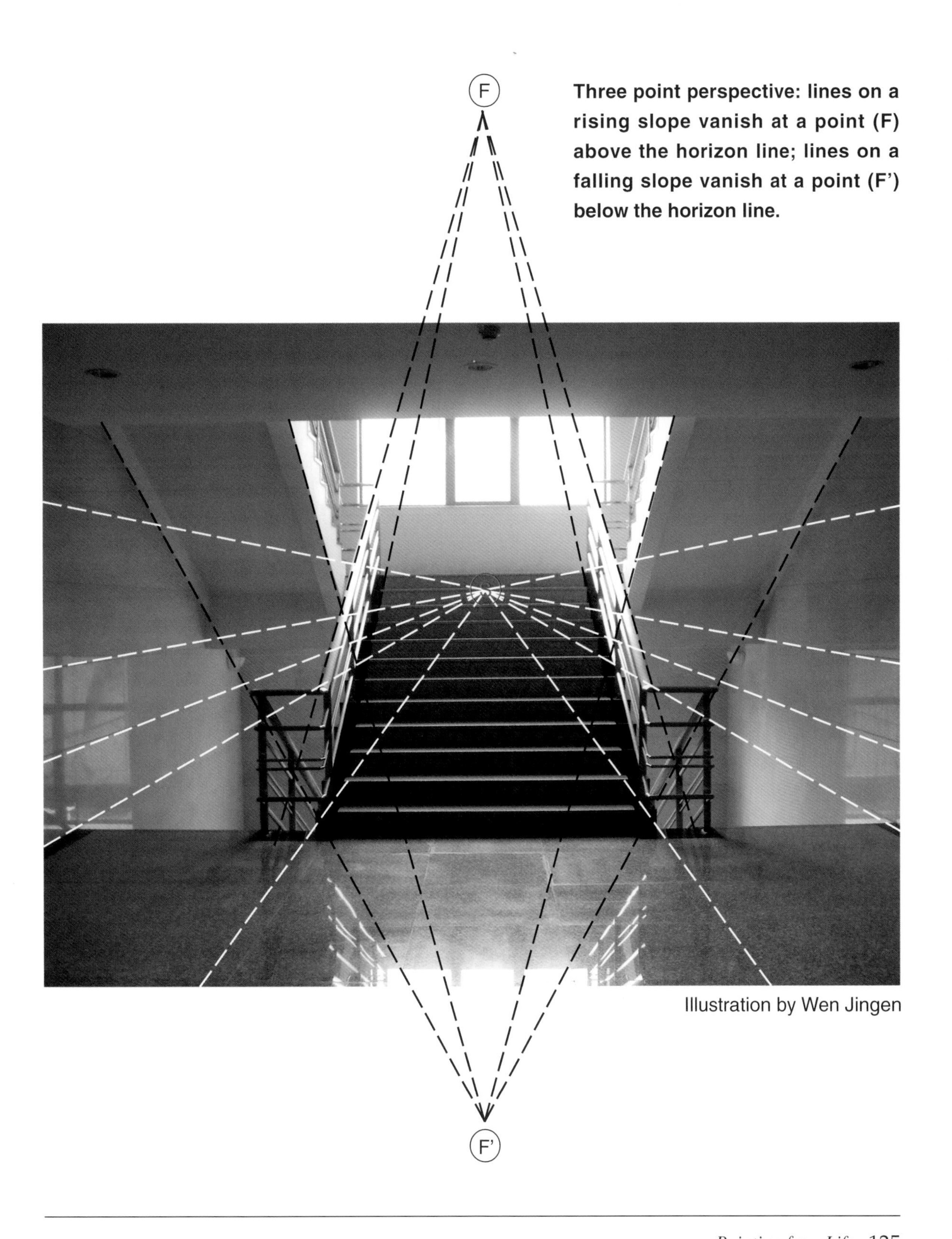

Three point perspective: lines on a rising slope vanish at a point (F) above the horizon line; lines on a falling slope vanish at a point (F') below the horizon line.

Illustration by Wen Jingen

This method is quite "precise". You can even mathematically work out the relative size of everything in a painting. However, it has advantages and limitations. The advantage is that it does help to create an illusion of depth on a flat surface (your painting) — you can go deep into it. Its limitation is that it constrains your view to a small area that does not represent what you have seen and what is stored in your memory. After you visit a beautiful mountain, equipped with a camera, you get a whole picture of the mountain in your head, but your camera only gives partial views. All the photos you have taken during the trip are "true" to life but none of them is true to your impression.

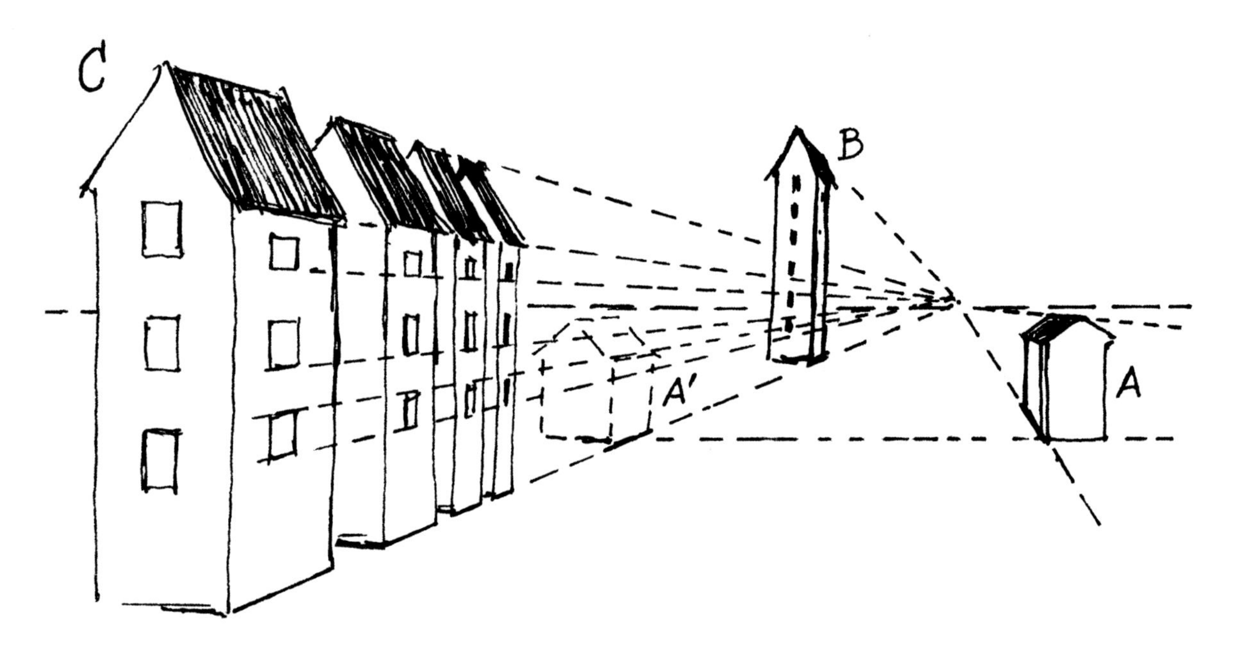

Illustration by Wen Jingen

Precise perspective: house A is half the height of house C. House B is double the height of house C.

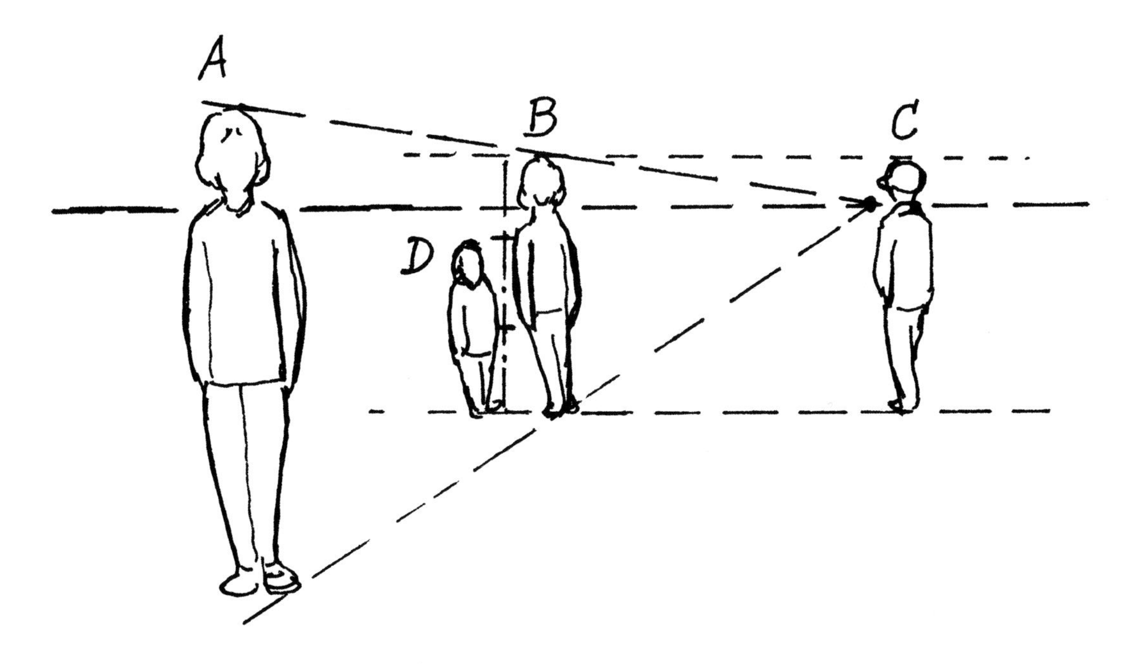

Illustration by Wen Jingen

Figures A, B and C are of equal height, Figure D is 2/3 the height of Figure A.

Chinese artists treat this problem in their own way. Their representation is not limited to one field of vision. They put many views into one picture thus exhibiting the whole picture stored in the artist's memory. Such a painting often has several focus points. A Chinese landscape artist can depict what he sees at eye level, above and below that level, and what he sees as he turns his head to the right, left or even further round. This method is called "scattered-focus" perspective (*sandian toushi* 散点[點]透视), as opposed to the Western true perspective. A Chinese landscape may be a two or three-metre high vertical scroll or a dozen-metre long horizontal scroll, and as the viewer unrolls the painting, he feels he is travelling among mountains or along a river with the artist. He is reliving the artist's experience. While you can view an oil painting all at once, you must view a Chinese scroll painting section by section.

Chinese artists' perspective is not as "precise" as in the West. Artists in China follow a few rough guidelines: the farther away an object is, the smaller it is; the nearer an object is, the larger it is. Everything has three surfaces. Nevertheless, with these few guidelines, Chinese landscape artists create extensive, imposing and enthralling pictures of nature.

A stone has three surfaces

Chinese artists believe that everything has three surfaces — the top, the front and a side. In landscape painting, this principle is applicable to depiction of stones and rocks. In Chinese landscape, the surfaces of a stone are not marked as distinctly as in Western drawing or painting, but Chinese artists pay close attention to arrangement of brushstrokes and ink. In Chinese painting the line is a means to display the form of objects. Shading is more to accentuate the structure of objects than a means to show light and shade in nature.

When depicting mountain ridges, Chinese artists pay close attention to the direction of the ridges, or "veins" (*mailuo* 脉络) as they are referred to.

A tree has branches extending in four directions

Though a tree can also have three surfaces, the treetop is not a solid cube and breaking the structure of a tree into three surfaces does not tally with people's visual habit. More aptly, artists recognise four directions into which the criss-cross branches of a tree extend: forward, backward, to the left and to the right. As the artist depicts the branches with fitting brushwork and ink washes, he pays more attention to the variation of density of the branches and leaves than the mechanical perspective of the branches.

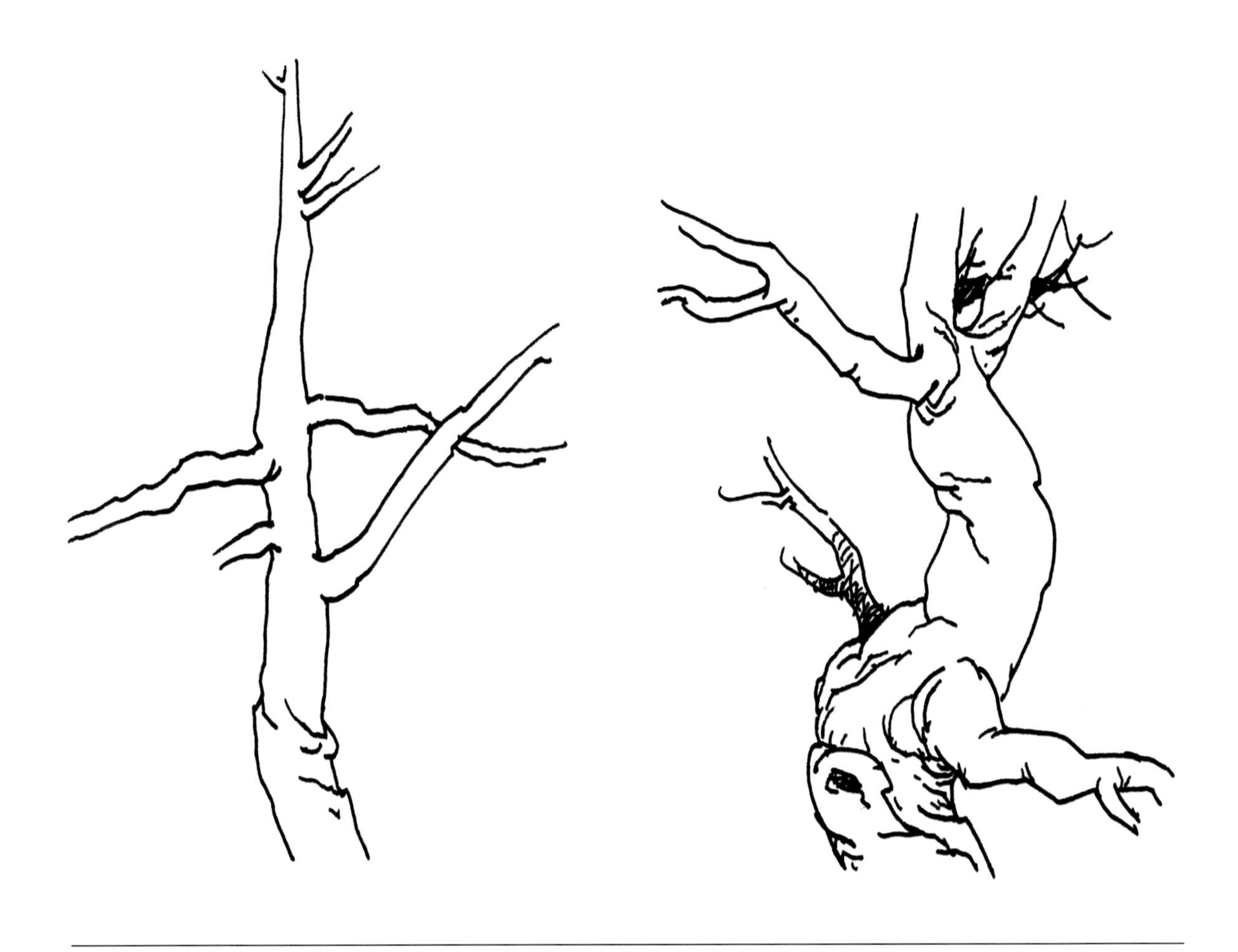

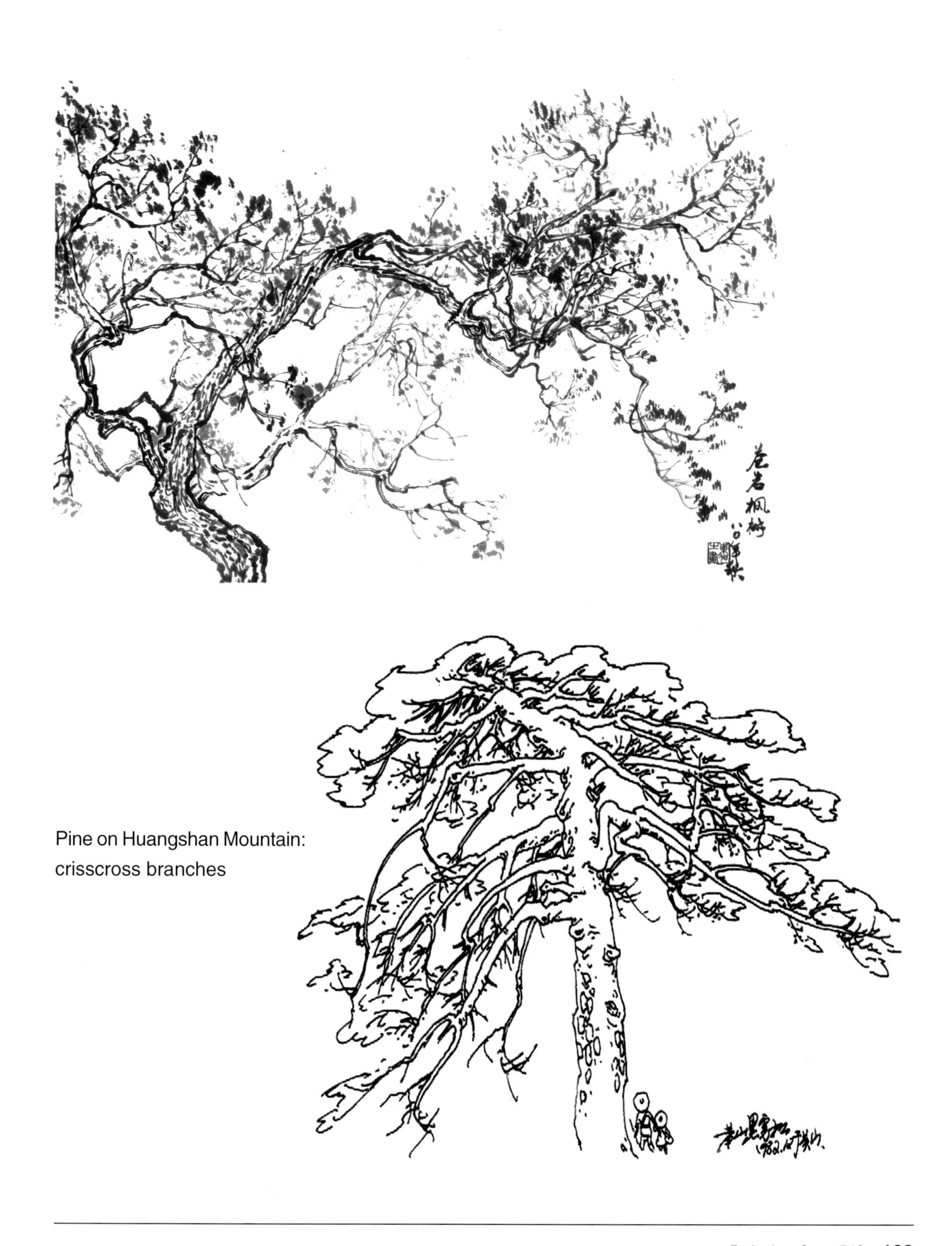

Pine on Huangshan Mountain:
crisscross branches

A broadleaf tree

Representation of seasons and time

Seasons. The characteristics of different seasons boil down to comparisons: smiling spring, dripping summer, dressed-up autumn and sleeping winter. Spring is compared to a smiling face because in spring everything comes to life and blooms in the warm breeze. In summer various plants are exuberant, rainfall is plentiful, brooks and rivers swell. That is why it is a dripping season. Autumn with splendid red and yellow leaves is as enchanting as a girl beautifully dressed up. In winter all tree became bare and the snow-covered land lays dormant. With these characteristics in mind, you will portray the seasons more successfully.

Warm Greenery in Spring Mountains by Yun Shouping (1633-1690)

Streams and Mountains in Summer by Sheng Mao (active 1320-1360)

Time. Few landscape artists depict noon or night scenes. Morning clouds and evening glow have been favourite themes. Morning views are usually tinted with a cool colour and evening scenes are often in a warm tone.

"Spirit" (*shen* 神) of mountains

To paint a mountain is like depicting a human being. Just as humans in their various forms have different personalities, mountains and rivers not only look different, but also have their own "souls" or dispositions. Chinese artists endeavour to manifest the spirit of everything through depiction of the forms. They believe that a good artwork must display formal and spiritual likeness at the same time. This principle does not only hold in figure painting, but in landscape as well. A mountain is not merely a heap of rocks. The geological structure and rock strata determine its form and "veins". Those factors give mountains each their own posture, airs and "spirit": some mountains stand towering, others extend into far distance, while yet more are perpendicular and perilous.

Chinese artists believe that only by realistic representation of the form of an object can the "spirit" of the subject be manifested, and that only by capturing the "spirit" of the object can the form be vivid and full of life. To achieve a representation that is both realistic and full of life, the artist should not only see the subject, but also observe and study the overall posture and general characteristics.

My sketches from life done at Huangshan, Yanshan, Gusai and Taihang mountains exemplify this principle.

Huangshan Mountains in central China are noted for the towering peaks, with ancient pines and grotesque rocks. Because the mountains stand in a humid zone, pines on the peaks strike roots into the fissures of rocks. A cornucopia of waterfalls flow down the rocks and clouds roll among peaks making a stunning picture of the mountains.

Yanshan Mountains north of Beijing are majestic with steep cliffs and brooks in deep dales, covered with trees.

This sketch shows a section of the ancient Great Wall built over mountains in Funing County, Hebei Province. In the precipitous mountains human beings are scarcely seen, yet in places zigzagging paths wind around mountains and a river runs through a pass. On the slopes stand huge rock columns.

This is a sketch from Taihang Mountains. In this mountain range most crags are bare and the veins of rocks are distinct and varied. Trees found there are largely persimmons, walnuts, and wild jujubes. With many watersheds in the mountains, brooks gurgle all the year through. In winter icicles are seen everywhere. The mountains are noted for their grandeur.

Vitality (*qi* 气[氣]). Spirit and vitality are very important yardsticks for excellent representation in Chinese painting. Vitality of a depiction comes from surety of the hand and from empathy with the subjects. This may sound abstract but through constant practice and viewing masterworks, you will learn to create impressive and energetic landscapes.

Creating a Landscape Painting

Composition

To produce a good landscape you must know something about composition. Chinese artists never include everything they see in their painting. They choose the beautiful things and arrange them according to some aesthetic principles. When expounding the aesthetic principle governing Chinese calligraphy, Chiang Yee said, "Asymmetry is a key word for Chinese composition". (*Chinese Calligraphy*, Harvard University Press, 1972 p. 220) This principle also holds for Chinese painting. While Western artists explain various types of composition with geometric forms like a triangle, a square or a circle, or some letters like A, S or V, Chinese artists use the metonymy of a lever — a pivot on which a beam turns. The longer arm with a small weight can achieve balance when used with the shorter arm and a greater weight. This figurative method better explains the unevenness in size, density, space and distance in a painting.

S composition

Triangle composition

Landscape by Huang Yi (1744-1802)

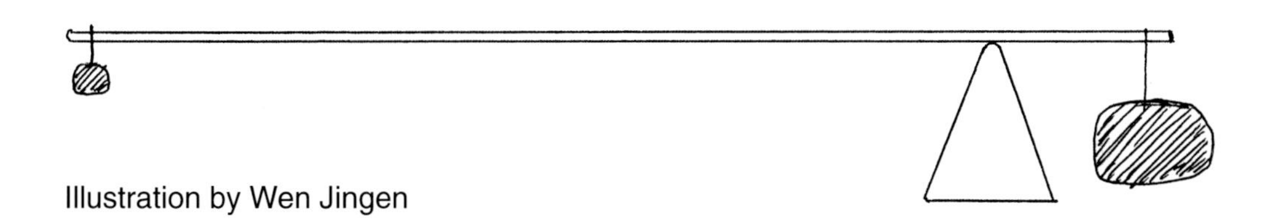

Illustration by Wen Jingen

Chinese landscape artists have reduced their experiences in artistic creation into one principle: openness and closeness. These two words also suggest beginning and end. This principle not only serves as a guideline for composition of a landscape painting, it is also useful for the appreciation of masterworks. With this principle in mind, you will know where to begin and where to end in the study of a landscape.

The elements for consideration are: beginning and end, host and guest, contending and conceding, amassing and dispersion, density and sparsity, frontal view and side view.

Beginning and end. Students of Chinese literature consider that a composition has its beginning, evolution, transition and conclusion. This also applies to Chinese landscape.

In the illustration ① indicates the beginning of the landscape; ② evolution of the motif; ③ the transition in the motif and ④ the conclusion.

Host and guest. Chinese art theorists compare some objects in a painting to a "host" and others to "guests". The "host" must be placed in an eye-catching position and the "guests" serve as a foil. In a landscape the host is usually a high peak and the guests are often lower mountains beside it and trees. The host and guests pose like friends greeting each other or an adult carrying an infant on his back. In case of the illustration, the tower is the host and the trees are guests.

Contending and conceding. As seen in the illustration, places marked as ① are where depicted objects (branches) contend to gain and places ② are where the branches yield. In nature plants tend to contend for sunshine and free space so as to facilitate their growth. Sometimes they struggle to gain a place and sometimes they gave way to each other. This relationship makes the brushwork rhythmic and interesting.

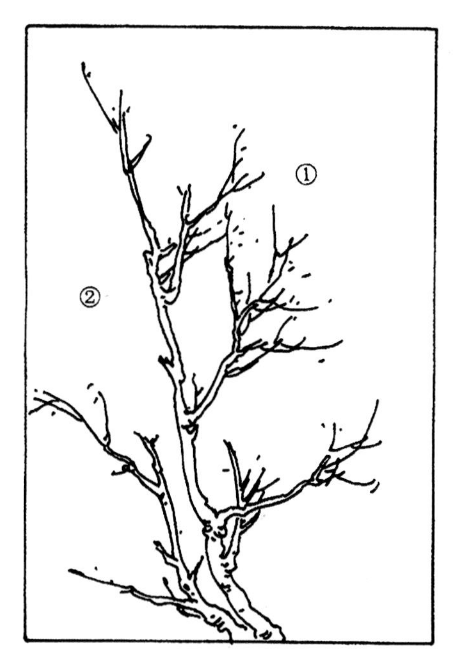

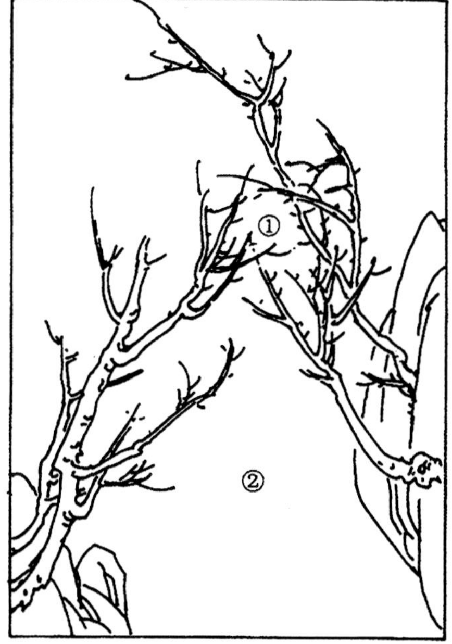

When porters meet on the road: comparison of brushstrokes in painting or calligraphy (担夫争[爭]道 *danfu zheng dao*)

The brushwork should be reasonably controlled. The texture-strokes in light ink should alternate with each other without disturbing each other, giving way to each other without clashing. Regarding calligraphy, ancient people compared brush strokes to porters with a shoulder pole vying with one another on the road. When porters meet on the road, with strong shoulders to carry loads, some of them walk to the left and others to the right, some in the front and others behind, so that they will not bump into each other. This is an excellent elucidation of brushwork. — Huang Binhong (1865-1955)

Density and sparsity. The composition of a painting may be dense or sparse. A sparsely composed painting may be suggestive and a densely composed painting may be full and exuberant. Also, in a painting some places may look denser than others. You can deliberately create a sparse composition or dense composition, but either composition should be coherent. It takes skill to unify separate images in a picture.

Landscape by Wang Zhirui (d.1657)

Sword Gate Pass by Huang Xiangjian (1609-1673)

More than three strokes crossing each other at one point or criss-crossing parallels lines look unsightly.

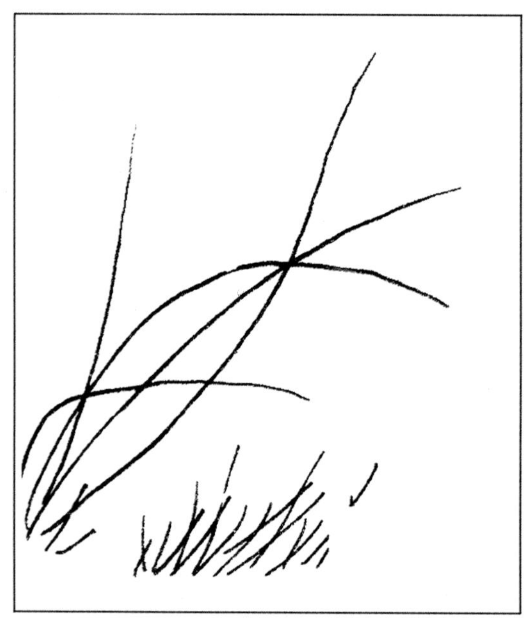

To avoid this, there are some guidelines.

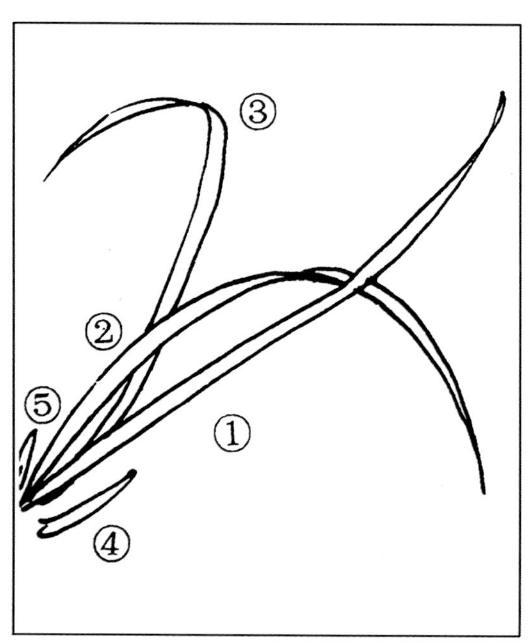

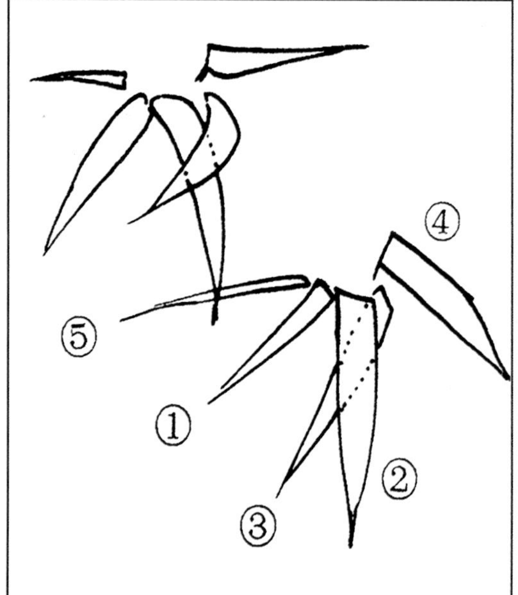

Frontal and side views. A portrait may present a person's frontal or side view. In a landscape or bird-and-flower painting, a frontal view of an object is achieved by putting the object in the centre of the painting and a side view is achieved by putting it on a side of the painting.

A frontal view of a mountain is grandiose and majestic.

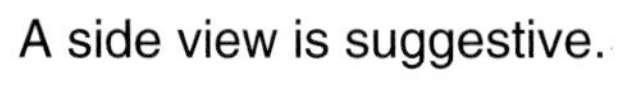

A side view is suggestive.

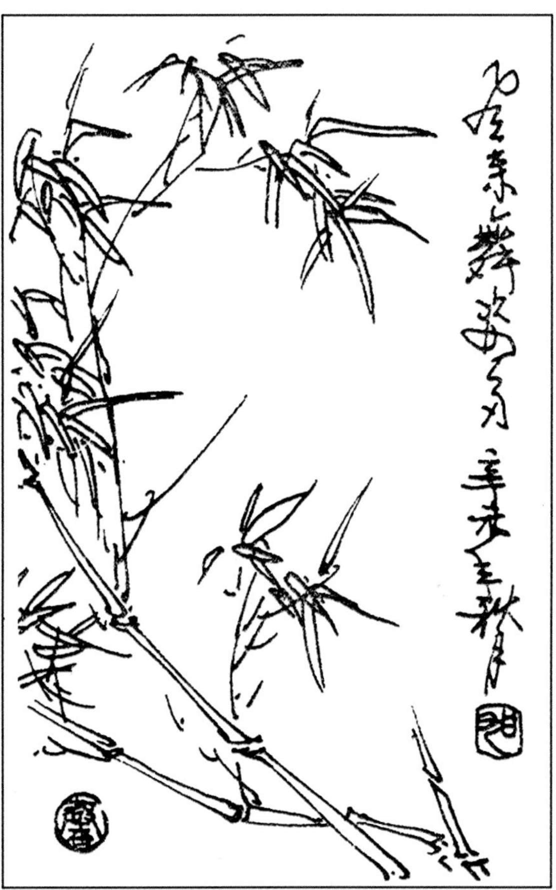

A painting may present the frontal view of some objects and side view of other.

Mountains and River in Autumn by Zhao Boju (attrib.)

Horizontal and vertical scroll formats. Chinese landscape is often done on a very long vertical or horizontal scroll. *Mountains and River in Autumn* attributed to Zhao Boju (active 1127-1162) is a long horizontal scroll. This masterpiece displays the veins of rocks and portrays concisely and vividly several human figures, houses, boats and carriages among a forest of peaks. It must have been the result of long lasting observation of life and artistic practice. The conscientiousness and meticulousness revealed in the masterly depiction sets an example for other artists.

The Hermit by Wei Xian (active sometime during the period 907-960) is a vertical scroll showing the ancient hermit Liang Hong and his wife Meng Guang living a simple life. An anecdote described that whenever Liang Hong returned home, his wife presented food by holding the tray at the level of her forehead, moving forward to the table on her knees. The groves and peaks in this well organised composition set off the lofty personality of the hermit.

Both in the past and today many Chinese artists have created paintings in formats other than extraordinarily long scrolls. Most paintings in exhibitions now are in formats much like the frames of oil paintings or watercolours.

Wildgeese Returning to Autumn Forest, 1880, by Wang Run.

Round and fan-shaped formats. Apart from vertical and horizontal scrolls, Chinese landscape can be painted on round, oval and folding fans. On a fan the "focus" of the painting must rest at the centre. Any inscription should be written along the folded sections, in a radiating manner. Vertical lines should also run along the folds so that the scene depicted on it looks natural, otherwise houses etc., will appear to be tilting.

Three ways to display distant views (*san yuan* 三远[遠])

Flat and distant: Extending distant view (*pingyuan* 平远[遠]). This is a view of a distant horizon with mountains and trees below eye level. It is a view of an artist standing on a very high place. We can also say it is a bird's-eye view with a high horizon line.

High and distant: Soaring distant view (*gaoyuan* 高远[遠]). This is an upward view with a low horizon line, which is usually blocked out of sight by mountains or other objects in the painting or even out of the painting. This form of composition is used to display high mountains.

Deep and distant: Diving distant view (*shenyuan* 深远[遠]). This composition is used to present cols, streams and paths in deep valleys. It is a combination of a perspective at eye level and a downward peep into deep valleys in the foreground.

Notable Masterpieces

Chinese landscape painting emerged before the Christian era and has undergone a long process of development. Instead of going deep into historical research, I have included some landscape masterworks. They are arranged chronologically, thus giving the reader a rough picture of the development. Please note that there are too many masters and masterpieces for us to present them all here in this book. To have a better understanding of Chinese landscape, I recommend that you read more books on the subject.

Kuanglu Mountain
by Jing Hao (active during the 10th century)

The painting shows the grandeur of the Kuanglu Mountain (present-day Lushan Mountain in central China) with clouds and mist hovering among its peaks. The artist Jing Hao summed up the experiences of earlier landscape artists and created his own personal style — noted for the wide panoramic view and the use of ink strokes as the main means of expression.

Xiaoxiang River (detail)
by Dong Yuan (d. circa AD 962)

Dong Yuan, a native of Nanjing, learnt blue-and-green landscape in his youth. Later he used ink strokes as the main mode of expression and painted long, thin and smooth strokes to shade rocks. His texture-strokes were painted like hemp-fibres followed by ink strokes on wet colour washes. With dots added, his landscapes portray the grace of southern China. Art historians characterise his works as exhibiting hills and mountains veiled by mist, bridges over streams with islets — all typical scenes in the south. This painting was executed with indigo and ink, with light ink dots on the hilltops suggesting the moist air of South China.

Travelling in Mountains by Fan Kuan (active 10th century)

Fan Kuan is the style name of Fan Zhongzheng (alternatively named Fan Zhongli), whose dates are unknown. "Kuan" in Chinese means "broad-minded" which described his personality, hence the appellation. One of the leading landscape artists of his time, he spent a long time studying nature and portraying different seasons. His paintings, usually of large size, are noted for towering rocks standing by rivers, and dense primitive forests on mountaintops. He liked to use dots to shade rocks. Few paintings of the 10th century are extant today but connoisseurs believe this is an authentic piece by Fan Kuan. The picture shows a scene in the region that is the present-day central Shaanxi near Xi'an. The towering peaks in a frontal view with exuberant trees are imposing. The light shade at the foot of the mountains provides an illusion of air. Fan Kuan's paintings are noted for vigorous brushwork and dark ink.

Rocks Against Horizon
by Guo Xi (c. 1023- c.1085)

Guo Xi was a favourite of the emperor. It was said that most paintings hanging in the imperial palace were his works. He was against following well trodden paths in art and advocated artistic creation by drawing inspiration from different masters and from the observation of life. He put forward the three ways to display distant views in landscape. This painting shows huge rocks against the horizon. His strokes are mostly centre-tip and side-tip brushwork in light ink.

Thousand Miles of Landscape (details)
by Wang Ximeng (12th century)

Wang Ximeng was a great master of blue-and-green landscape. His dates are unknown, but we do know he worked for the emperor during the reign of Zhenghe (1111-1118). Historical documents say that he was once taught by the artist-emperor, but this prodigious artist died young. This is the only extant work attributed to him.

Walking While Singing
by Ma Yuan (12-13th century)

The exact dates of this artist are unknown, but we do know that he served in the imperial painting academy during the period 1190-1224. The all-around master Ma Yuan excelled in landscape, human figure and bird-and-flower paintings. A salient feature of his landscape work was breaking with the earlier tradition of panoramic views. In his painting he focused on one aspect of nature and for this he acquired the nickname "One Corner Ma" (*ma yijiao* 马[馬]一角). This style exerted a great influence on later artists. He liked to use large axe-cut strokes to depict rocks and was also good at portraying water. His "Walking While Singing" shows drunken farmers and children playing along a path. The peaks in the background are steep and rocks are depicted with long, forceful and angular strokes. The mist and clouds veiling part of trees set off the light and space in the sky. This painting impresses viewers with its forceful brushwork and graceful images.

Serene Mountains and River (details)
by Xia Gui (12-13th century)

Xia Gui, whose exact dates are also unknown, may have lived a little later than Ma Yuan. He served in the imperial painting academy between AD 1195 and 1224. He excelled in both landscape and human figure. He loved to depict rivers in wind, rain, snow and mist in southern China. He produced many extraordinarily long scrolls. His "Serene Mountains and River" is a 33-metre horizontal scroll. Xia Gui's style is akin to that of Ma Yuan, and both artists had a propensity for simple composition and long axe-cut strokes. But Xia's landscapes have a milder tone than Ma's — while Ma Yuan outlined tree leaves, Xia Gui depicted his tree leaves with dots. He also loved to apply texture-strokes with a blunt brush and to add ink marks on the texture-strokes, thus achieving a brilliant symphony of wet and dry, dark and light. The "Serene Mountains and River" displays a brilliant scene with an expanse of water in the background and mountains in the foreground. The light strokes on the trees give a feeling of air and space. The neat and fresh brushwork impresses the viewer with a beauty contained in simplicity.

Autumn in Queshan and Huashan Mountains (detail)
by Zhao Mengfu (1254-1322)

This artist was one of the most influential calligraphers and painters during the reign of the Mongols in China. He had two important views. One was that good art must possess "ancient flavours" and the other, that brushwork used in painting and calligraphy is the same. His theory encouraged artistic creation by copying ancient works. But on the other hand he also stressed artwork as an expression of nature. His works appear in various guises — some of his landscapes are very sketchy, but his human figures and horses are meticulously executed and brilliantly coloured. The "Autumn in Queshan and Huashan Mountains" is a magnum opus of Zhao.

Dwelling in the Fuchun Mountains (detail)
by Huang Gongwang (1269-1354)

Huang Gongwang once served in the government as a minor clerk but was later prosecuted and thrown into prison. Upon being freed, he returned home and concentrated all his efforts on landscape painting. He sat amongst rocks in the woods for a whole day, observing nature and often sketched from life. Huang used dry texture-strokes and skimming strokes. He inherited the tradition of landscape ink painting from former masters and strove to achieve variation in brushwork. He applied a light red colour to his landscape and this format was later known as the "light-red landscape". The scroll, 33 cm in height and 670 cm in length, displays hamlets and forests in spring along the Fuchun River. The wet hemp-fibre stroke, long and short dry strokes mixed with wet dots make the painting an epitome of varied brushwork. On the other hand, too much attention focused on brushwork tends to reduce the natural appeal of the spring sight.

Cold Pines in Valley
by Ni Zan (1301-1374)

This artist enjoyed a reputation for his aloofness from politics and mundane affairs. His paintings without human figures have been praised for their appeal hidden in sparse and simple brushwork. The trees, distant peaks, flat mounds and wild waters depicted in light strokes imbue the whole picture with a desolate atmosphere. The brushwork and the inscription suggest that this was done in the artist's later years.

Houses in the Forest on Juqu Lake by Wang Meng (d. 1385)

Juqu Lake was the old name for Taihu Lake in Jiangsu Province in eastern China. Wang Meng was one of the leading artists when Mongols ruled China. He studied the masters of earlier times and developed his style of dense brushwork and compacted composition, as exemplified by this picture. The painting, filled with rocks, trees and thatched houses amongst the trees, has little breathing space except in the stream. This full composition was an innovation in the history of Chinese landscape painting. The tiny figures among rocks and along paths permeate it with a scent of life. Rocks in this painting were executed with the dry "ox-hair" and "loosened strands" strokes. The sinuous lines contouring the rocks show the characteristic rock formation in the region of Taihu Lake. In China such rocks are often used to build rock gardens.

The High Mountain Lushan by Shen Zhou (1427-1509)

Shen Zhou and his followers were called the Wu School or Wumen School (Wu or Wumen being the region where he lived — near present-day Shanghai and Nanjing), an orthodox literati painting school during his time. He was skilled in using vigorous, thick centre-tip strokes and his compositions were unique. This grandiose painting is executed in precise brushwork. A waterfall jumping down high rocks seems to gurgle on. Trees in the mountain are depicted with neat strokes. The whole picture treats the viewer to the charm of Lushan Mountain.

Refined Conversation under Trees
by Wen Zhengming (1470-1559)

A noted poet, calligrapher and painter, Wen Zhengming had dozens of students and offspring who followed his art. It is said during his later years, customers who came for his paintings put piles of paper on his desk. He emphasised the flavour of brush-work and employed thin, sturdy, neat and dense strokes. Many of his works had literary taste but some of his paintings lacked strength and appeared dull and dry. Apart from landscape Wen Zhengming also produced bird-and-flower paintings and figures. His works are in two styles, some meticulously done while others free hand, hence the names "Meticulous Wen" and "Sketchy Wen". This painting belongs to Wen's meticulous style.

Villages after Rain
by Wen Zhengming

This painting illustrates Wen Zhengming's other style — free-hand.

Fairyland at the Source of Peach Blossom Stream by Qiu Ying (d. 1552)

Qiu Ying was a contemporary of Wen Zhengming and also a member of the Wu or Wumen School. Of all the artists of this school, technically, Qiu Ying was the most professional one. He made a living by selling his own paintings. His brushwork was smooth, neat and at the same time vigorous and forceful. He used brilliant colours. Unlike other literati artists, Qiu Ying did not add garrulous inscriptions to his paintings.

Willows on the Bank and a River Boat by Wang Hui (1632-1717)

Wang Hui is a representative of the artists who paid more attention to copying ancient masters than depicting the real life.

Snow Scene
by Shi Tao (1636-1710)

Once a member of the imperial family, Shi Tao became a Buddhist monk after the dynasty of his family fell to the Manchu conquerors. He visited many famous mountains and rivers, and also drew inspiration from nature. The author of *Quotations from Shi Tao*, a summary of his lifelong artistic creation, he held that one should learn from ancient masters only in order to bring forth new art. "Brushwork and ink application should keep pace with the time" was his maxim. He advocated innovation in art. Most of his landscape paintings were done from life. His bold compositions broke with set formats, showing the uniqueness of the subjects and his own feelings. His brushwork is unrestrained, luxurious and robust.

Serene Lotus in Summer Resort by Yuan Jiang (1662-1735)

This painting belongs to the genre called ruled-line painting (*jiehua* 界画 [畫]). This genre takes buildings as its motif and is executed with the help of a special ruler technique. During the period from the 7th to 10th century, this genre reached the height of its maturity. But after the 14th century, many literati artists disdained it as being of "low taste". Today we know that this was unfair but during many centuries this genre was neglected and few artists turned their attention to it. At a time when the ruled-line painting was at the brink of extinction, Yuan Jiang and his nephew Yuan Yao devoted their lives to the preservation of this genre of painting. Commendably, their efforts and creativity salvaged a tradition. The painting shows a summer resort of some idle rich man. The meandering pathways, groves of trees, bamboo and the mirror-like water make the viewer feel the soothing summer breeze. Yuan Jiang was also a good figure painter.

Ten Villas (detail)
by Ren Xiong (1823-1857)

Ren Xiong was an outstanding master and adaptable painter. He, his brother Ren Xun and his nephew, Ren Yu, together with Ren Yi exerted a great influence on Shanghai artists during the latter part of the 19th century and the early part of the 20th century. This album leaf shows his achievement in blue-and-green landscape.

Landscape
by Xu Gu (1824-1896)

At a time when calligraphic brushwork played an important part in painting, Xu Gu blazed a new trail by employing side-tip strokes and rhythmic ink shades, as exemplified by this leaf from an album.

Landscape
by Wu Changshuo (1844-1927)

In the 19th century the "mainstream" painting had become rather "calligraphic". Many Chinese painters applied what they achieved from the study of ancient writing and calligraphy to their work and thus the brushwork in their paintings became rather calligraphic, as illustrated by this painting.

驚蟄
丁丑秋
林凡

Early Spring by Lin Fan (b. 1931)

Landscape by Huang Binhong (1865-1955)

Huang Binhong, a great figure of 20th-century Chinese art, took care to study early masterpieces, particularly those carried out during the period from the 11th century to the 15th century. He attached great importance to traditional brushwork and ink application, trying to achieve simplicity and exuberance in his creation, as exemplified by this painting. He is a great exponent of tradition and at the same time a courageous innovator.

Soul of China

The scroll, 1 m. in height and 54 m. in length, displays China's Great Wall in 25 sections from right to left. It was created in eight years from 1981. To gather visual materials for my creation, I travelled thousands of miles on foot to make sketches of the Great Wall, often passing the night in the company of wild animals. The Great Wall was built with 180 million cubic metres of earth plus 60 million cubic metres of stones and bricks. It is a one of the Wonders of the World. In depicting the Great Wall, I considered the brushwork, application of ink and colour, doing my utmost to capture its grandeur and majesty. The painting is an ode which I dedicate to the Great Wall, the soul of China, and to the Chinese nation.

4. Shanhai Pass; 3. Temple to Meng Jiangnü, a legendary woman whose husband died during construction of the Great Wall. She cried at the site, causing a section of the wall to collapse.

8. Perilous peaks; 7. Pastoral song

12. Red fruit in blue mountains; 11. Badaling Pass

2. Bohai Gulf; 1. Old dragon's head

6. Lazikou (Huge rock) Pass; 5. Qingshi (Blue stone) Valley

10. Beacon tower; 9. Gold-mountain castle

16. Evening clouds above valleys; 15. Dragon over natural abyss

20. Red trees; 19. Rock walls and deep valleys

24. Jiayu Pass; 23. Camels with tinkling bells in desert

14. Towers on purple rocks; 13. Evening glow at ancient wall

18. Waterfalls after snow; 17. Green peaks

22. Sunset in winter; 21. Mist veiled green mountains

25. Sandy wind in Gobi desert

Appendix

Tricks - painting with instruments other than the brush

The brush and ink have been regarded as the basic instruments of Chinese painting, but sometimes other devices can be used as well. Historical documents have records of some ancient artists who produced original paintings with fingertips, lotus pods, twigs, etc.

Earliest record about paintings tricks

It is said that during the reign of Qinshihuang (the first Chinese emperor who unified China in 221 BC), an envoy from Tengxiao (in Central Asia) gave the emperor tribute and produced paintings for him by spraying colour from his mouth onto walls. The colours on walls became lifelike images of birds, animals and landscape. This may be the earliest record about paintings tricks in China.

Nowadays many Chinese artists make daring experiments with new devices and instruments. Some traditionally minded artists and art theorists play down or are against such efforts. In my opinion, special skills can be used but they should only be used as an accessory or to compliment the painting. Special skills like creasing or wrinkling paper do produce interesting effects that are not achievable with ordinary means, but such effects are rather "accidental" — giving both desirable and undesired effects.

Creasing paper. When shaded or brushed with ink or colour, creased or wrinkled unsized paper produces wet and dry, or light and dark marks on the raised areas. A large wrinkled area may serve as a ground for further colouring or strokes. The rough surface of certain objects like the trunk of an old tree or a pile of bare rocks may be better depicted if the relative areas on the paper are creased. You will need to flatten your finished painting — spray with water, stroke it out to an even smoothness and leave to dry.

Dropping alum liquid. Dissolve alum (it usually comes as a white powder) into water and place drops of this liquid onto unsized paper. Because alum is resistant to ink and colour, painting on this paper afterwards gives interesting effects. Experiment with making marks onto the alum paper while it is still damp or again when it has dried completely. Snowflakes, raindrops, spots on tree trunks and such things can be portrayed. You may also mix colour into the alum liquid.

Spraying water on your painting. You may spray water before or after ink is applied. You may also spray your saliva onto paper and paint over it.

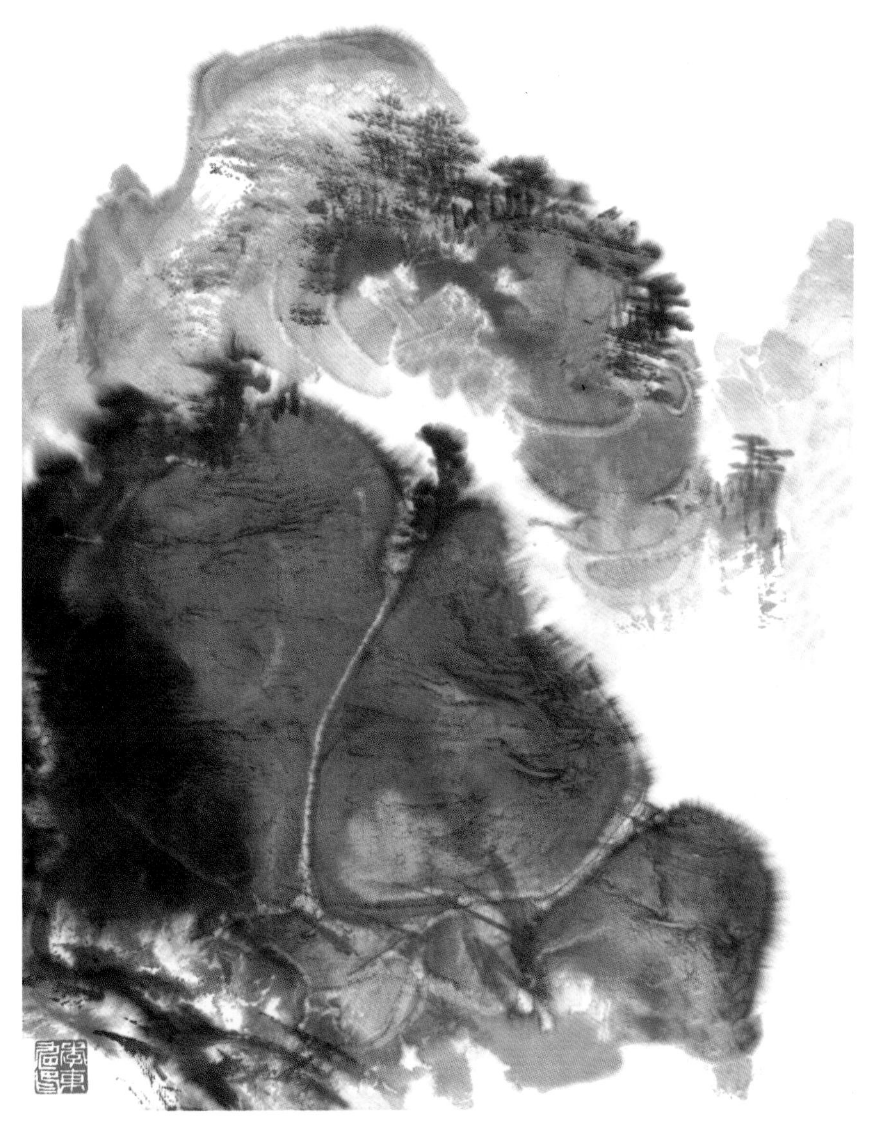

Blotting. Brush, drop, pour ink or colour, or both, onto a smooth surface like glass or a worktop. Do not cover the whole surface with evenly shaded ink or colour. Some areas may be darker than others and some places may be left dry. It is better to conceive a rough outline of a picture before you apply ink or colour. Lower a piece of unsized paper onto the surface. Lift the paper, leave it dry and you will see some recognisable images on it. Elaborate on the "images" to achieve an excellent painting with surprising results.

"Rubbing" from water surface. Pour ink into a basin of clear water and stir the water. When irregular whorls of streaks appear, put a piece of unsized paper flatly onto the surface of water and lift it adeptly. Put the wet paper on a sheet of clean paper and leave it dry. When the wet paper becomes dry, work into it further to complete a painting.

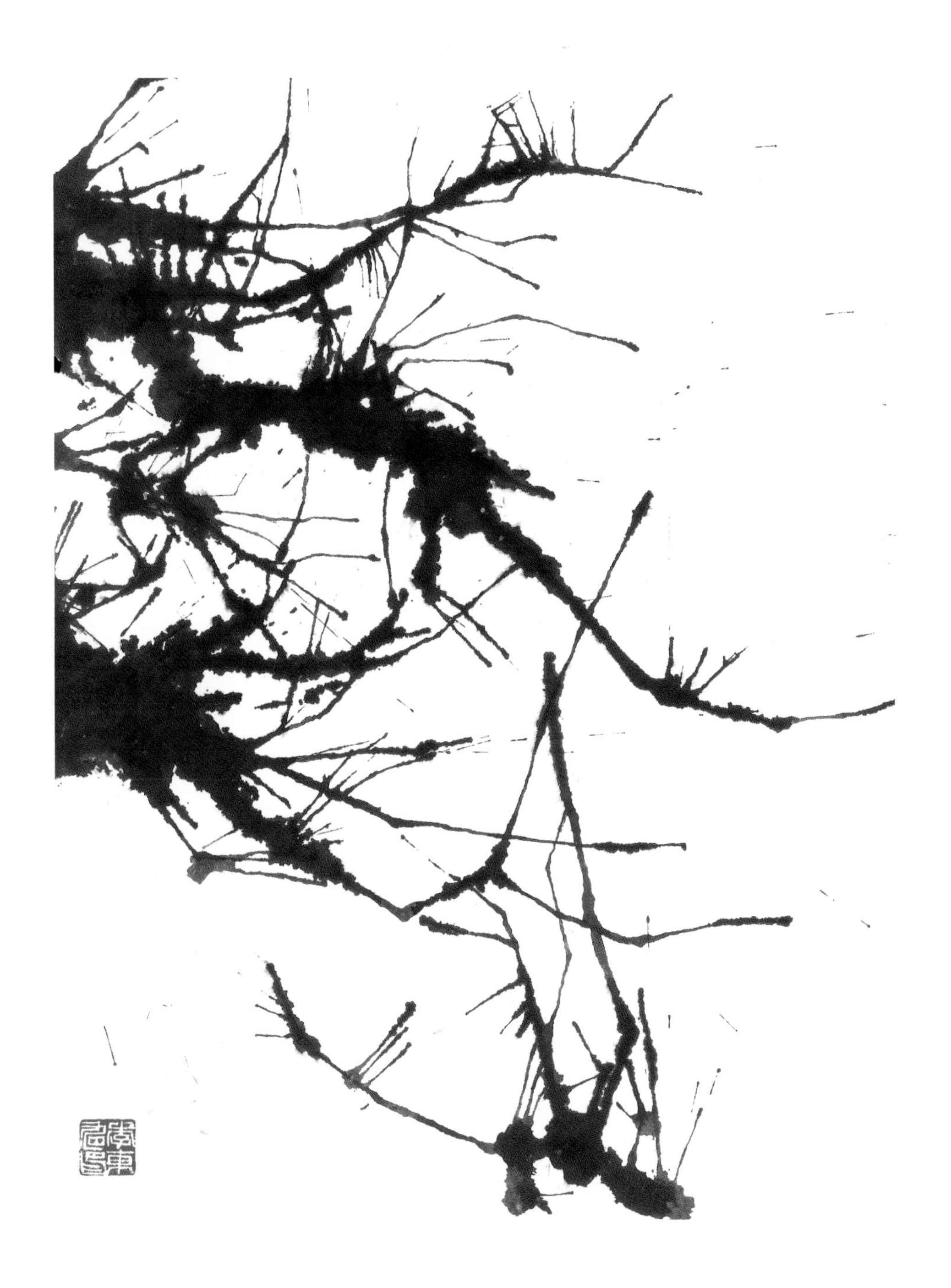

Blowing. Drop ink onto sized paper and blow on the ink drops. This produces special traces like holes on worm-eaten timber or raindrops on an old wall. This technique is good for the depiction of tree branches.

图书在版编目（CIP）数据

怎样画山水画 / 李东旭编著，温晋根编译.
－北京：外文出版社，2006
(怎样做系列)
ISBN 978-7-119-04615-0

I. 怎... II. ①李...②温... III. 山水画—技法(美术) — 英文 IV. J212.26

中国版本图书馆 CIP 数据核字（2006）第 114480 号

责任编辑　温晋根
封面设计　蔡　荣
插图绘制　李东旭，温晋根，孙树明

外文出版社网址:
http://www.flp.com.cn
外文出版社电子信箱:
info@flp.com.cn
sales@flp.com.cn

怎样画山水画

李东旭 著

*

外文出版社出版
(中国北京百万庄大街 24 号
邮政编码 100037)
北京雷杰印刷有限公司印刷
中国国际图书贸易总公司发行
(中国北京车公庄西路 35 号
北京邮政信箱第 399 号　邮政编码 100044)
2007 年(16 开)第 1 版
2007 年第 1 版第 1 次印刷
2009 年 6 月第 1 版第 2 次印刷
(英)
ISBN 978-7-119-04615-0
15000(平)
7-E-3757P